2016 SQA Past Papers With Answers

National 5
MODERN STUDIES

2014, 2015 & 2016 Exams

HODDER
GIBSON
AN HACHETTE UK COMPANY

This book contains the official SQA 2014, 2015 and 2016 Exams for National 5 Modern Studies, with associated SQA-approved answers modified from the official marking instructions that accompany the paper.

In addition the book contains skills advice. This advice has been specially commissioned by Hodder Gibson, and has been written by experienced senior teachers and examiners in line with the new National 5 syllabus and assessment outlines. This is not SQA material but has been devised to provide further guidance for National 5 examinations.

Hodder Gibson is grateful to the copyright holders, as credited on the final page of the Answer Section, for permission to use their material. Every effort has been made to trace the copyright holders and to obtain their permission for the use of copyright material. Hodder Gibson will be happy to receive information allowing us to rectify any error or omission in future editions.

Hachette UK's policy is to use papers that are natural, renewable and recyclable products and made from wood grown in sustainable forests. The logging and manufacturing processes are expected to conform to the environmental regulations of the country of origin.

Orders: please contact Bookpoint Ltd, 130 Park Drive, Milton Park, Abingdon, Oxon OX14 4SE. Telephone: (44) 01235 827720. Fax: (44) 01235 400454. Lines are open 9.00–5.00, Monday to Saturday, with a 24-hour message answering service. Visit our website at www.hoddereducation.co.uk. Hodder Gibson can be contacted direct on: Tel: 0141 333 4650; Fax: 0141 404 8188; email: hoddergibson@hodder.co.uk

This collection first published in 2016 by
Hodder Gibson, an imprint of Hodder Education,
An Hachette UK Company
211 St Vincent Street
Glasgow G2 5QY

Typeset by Aptara, Inc.

Printed in the UK

A catalogue record for this title is available from the British Library

ISBN: 978-1-4718-9117-5

3 2 1

2017 2016

Introduction

Study Skills – what you need to know to pass exams!

Pause for thought

Many students might skip quickly through a page like this. After all, we all know how to revise. Do you really though?

Think about this:

"IF YOU ALWAYS DO WHAT YOU ALWAYS DO, YOU WILL ALWAYS GET WHAT YOU HAVE ALWAYS GOT."

Do you like the grades you get? Do you want to do better? If you get full marks in your assessment, then that's great! Change nothing! This section is just to help you get that little bit better than you already are.

There are two main parts to the advice on offer here. The first part highlights fairly obvious things but which are also very important. The second part makes suggestions about revision that you might not have thought about but which WILL help you.

Part 1

DOH! It's so obvious but …

Start revising in good time

Don't leave it until the last minute – this will make you panic.

Make a revision timetable that sets out work time AND play time.

Sleep and eat!

Obvious really, and very helpful. Avoid arguments or stressful things too – even games that wind you up. You need to be fit, awake and focused!

Know your place!

Make sure you know exactly **WHEN and WHERE** your exams are.

Know your enemy!

Make sure you know what to expect in the exam.

How is the paper structured?

How much time is there for each question?

What types of question are involved?

Which topics seem to come up time and time again?

Which topics are your strongest and which are your weakest?

Are all topics compulsory or are there choices?

Learn by DOING!

There is no substitute for past papers and practice papers – they are simply essential! Tackling this collection of papers and answers is exactly the right thing to be doing as your exams approach.

Part 2

People learn in different ways. Some like low light, some bright. Some like early morning, some like evening / night. Some prefer warm, some prefer cold. But everyone uses their BRAIN and the brain works when it is active. Passive learning – sitting gazing at notes – is the most INEFFICIENT way to learn anything. Below you will find tips and ideas for making your revision more effective and maybe even more enjoyable. What follows gets your brain active, and active learning works!

Activity 1 – Stop and review

Step 1

When you have done no more than 5 minutes of revision reading STOP!

Step 2

Write a heading in your own words which sums up the topic you have been revising.

Step 3

Write a summary of what you have revised in no more than two sentences. Don't fool yourself by saying, "I know it, but I cannot put it into words". That just means you don't know it well enough. If you cannot write your summary, revise that section again, knowing that you must write a summary at the end of it. Many of you will have notebooks full of blue/black ink writing. Many of the pages will not be especially attractive or memorable so try to liven them up a bit with colour as you are reviewing and rewriting. **This is a great memory aid, and memory is the most important thing.**

Activity 2 – Use technology!

Why should everything be written down? Have you thought about "mental" maps, diagrams, cartoons and colour to help you learn? And rather than write down notes, why not record your revision material?

What about having a text message revision session with friends? Keep in touch with them to find out how and what they are revising and share ideas and questions.

Why not make a video diary where you tell the camera what you are doing, what you think you have learned and what you still have to do? No one has to see or hear it, but the process of having to organise your thoughts in a formal way to explain something is a very important learning practice.

Be sure to make use of electronic files. You could begin to summarise your class notes. Your typing might be slow, but it will get faster and the typed notes will be easier to read than the scribbles in your class notes. Try to add different fonts and colours to make your work stand out. You can easily Google relevant pictures, cartoons and diagrams which you can copy and paste to make your work more attractive and **MEMORABLE**.

Activity 3 – This is it. Do this and you will know lots!

Step 1

In this task you must be very honest with yourself! Find the SQA syllabus for your subject (www.sqa.org.uk). Look at how it is broken down into main topics called MANDATORY knowledge. That means stuff you MUST know.

Step 2

BEFORE you do ANY revision on this topic, write a list of everything that you already know about the subject. It might be quite a long list but you only need to write it once. It shows you all the information that is already in your long-term memory so you know what parts you do not need to revise!

Step 3

Pick a chapter or section from your book or revision notes. Choose a fairly large section or a whole chapter to get the most out of this activity.

With a buddy, use Skype, Facetime, Twitter or any other communication you have, to play the game "If this is the answer, what is the question?". For example, if you are revising Geography and the answer you provide is "meander", your buddy would have to make up a question like "What is the word that describes a feature of a river where it flows slowly and bends often from side to side?".

Make up 10 "answers" based on the content of the chapter or section you are using. Give this to your buddy to solve while you solve theirs.

Step 4

Construct a wordsearch of at least 10 × 10 squares. You can make it as big as you like but keep it realistic. Work together with a group of friends. Many apps allow you to make wordsearch puzzles online. The words and phrases can go in any direction and phrases can be split. Your puzzle must only contain facts linked to the topic you are revising. Your task is to find 10 bits of information to hide in your puzzle, but you must not repeat information that you used in Step 3. DO NOT show where the words are. Fill up empty squares with random letters. Remember to keep a note of where your answers are hidden but do not show your friends. When you have a complete puzzle, exchange it with a friend to solve each other's puzzle.

Step 5

Now make up 10 questions (not "answers" this time) based on the same chapter used in the previous two tasks. Again, you must find NEW information that you have not yet used. Now it's getting hard to find that new information! Again, give your questions to a friend to answer.

Step 6

As you have been doing the puzzles, your brain has been actively searching for new information. Now write a NEW LIST that contains only the new information you have discovered when doing the puzzles. Your new list is the one to look at repeatedly for short bursts over the next few days. Try to remember more and more of it without looking at it. After a few days, you should be able to add words from your second list to your first list as you increase the information in your long-term memory.

FINALLY! Be inspired...

Make a list of different revision ideas and beside each one write **THINGS I HAVE** tried, **THINGS I WILL** try and **THINGS I MIGHT** try. Don't be scared of trying something new.

And remember – "FAIL TO PREPARE AND PREPARE TO FAIL!"

National 5 Modern Studies

The course

You will have studied the following three units:

- Democracy in Scotland and the United Kingdom
- Social Issues in the United Kingdom
- International Issues

Your teacher will usually have chosen one topic from each of the 3 sections above and you will answer questions on these in your exam (see table below).

SECTION 1	CHOICE ONE	CHOICE TWO
Democracy in Scotland and UK	A Democracy in Scotland	**OR** B Democracy in the UK
SECTION 2	CHOICE ONE	CHOICE TWO
Social Issues in the UK	C Social Inequality	**OR** D Crime and the Law
SECTION 3	CHOICE ONE	CHOICE TWO
International Issues	E World Powers	**OR** F World Issues

The Added Value unit for National 5 is an externally marked assessment. This consists of two parts:

- National 5 question paper
  60 marks allocated
  75% of marks
- National 5 assignment
  20 marks allocated
  25% of marks

Total marks available = 80

To gain the course award, all units and course assessments must be passed. The marks you achieve in the question paper and assignment are added together and an overall mark will indicate a pass or fail. From this, your course award will then be graded.

Question paper

You will have 1 hour and 30 minutes to complete the question paper, with a total of 60 marks allocated. There are 26 marks available for skills-based questions and 34 for knowledge and understanding, with 20 marks in total for each of the three exam sections as outlined in the table above.

In the exam paper, more marks are awarded for knowledge and understanding than skills so it is crucial that you have a sound grasp of content.

As stated, the paper will be divided into three sections, each worth 20 marks. Each section will have three questions. The three questions will be as follows:

Describe (worth either 4, 6 or 8 marks)
For example:

> Describe, in detail, at least two ways in which the police try to reduce crime levels.

Explain (worth either 4, 6 or 8 marks)
For example:

> Explain, in detail, why many people in the UK have good health while others do not.

Source-based (worth either out of 8 or 10)
For example:

> Using Sources 1, 2 and 3, what conclusions can be drawn about…?

What types of source-based questions will I need to answer?

There are three types of source-based skills questions and you will have practised these as class work. These three source-based skills questions are as follows:

- Using sources of information to identify and explain selective use of facts – this will have been assessed in your **Democracy in Scotland and UK unit**
- Using sources of information to make and justify a decision – this will have been assessed in your **Social Issues in the UK unit**
- Using sources of information to draw and support conclusions – this will have been assessed in your **International Issues unit.**

Remember, in your course exam the skills based questions can appear in any of the three units – so selective use of facts could be a question in the International Issues section of the exam.

Remember, in your course exam the knowledge and skills questions for International Issues will not refer to a particular country or issue. You will be expected to base your describe and explain answers around your knowledge and understanding of the World Power or World Issue you have studied.

What makes a good Knowledge and Understanding answer?

- Answer the question as set and only provide information relevant to the question.
- As far as you can, use up-to-date examples to illustrate your understanding of the question.

- Answer in detail and write in paragraphs with development of the points you wish to discuss. Remember, one very developed describe answer can gain 3 marks and one very developed explain answer can gain 4 marks.

- Show awareness of the difference between **describe** and **explain** questions and be able to answer appropriately.

- Use the number of marks given to each question as a guide to how much to write. Writing a long answer for a four mark question may cause you difficulty in completing the paper.

What makes a bad Knowledge and Understanding answer?

- Don't just write a list of facts. You will receive a maximum of two marks.

- Don't change the question to what you know – this is called *turning a question* and you will receive no marks for detailed description or explanation if it is not relevant.

- Avoid giving answers that are dated and too historical. This is especially a danger in the International Issues section.

- Don't rush together different issues, factors and explanations without developing your answer.

What makes a good Skills answer?

- Make full use of all the sources by linking evidence from more than one source to provide detailed arguments.

- Interpret statistical sources to indicate their significance to a question and how they link to other evidence.

- Make sure you use only the sources provided when writing your answers.

What makes a bad Skills answer?

- Don't use only a single piece of evidence from a source to provide argument.

- Don't simply repeat the statistical or written evidence without indicating its significance.

- Avoid bringing in your own knowledge of the issue or your own personal opinion.

Specific Skills advice

- For a selective use of facts answer, you should state whether the evidence being used is showing selectivity or not, and whether the evidence is supporting or opposing the view.

- For a conclusion answer, you should use the headings to draw an overall conclusion, which may be given at the beginning or end of the explanation.

- For a decision/recommendation answer, you should justify your decision and explain why you have rejected the other option.

Main Changes to Course Content

Democracy in Scotland and the United Kingdom

A study of the media is no longer optional and you must investigate the following:

- the impact of the media on election and democracy in Scotland or in the UK

- the case study choice is now either pressure groups or trade unions and their impact on elections and democracy in Scotland or in the UK

You will also examine the role of political parties in election campaigns in Scotland or in the UK in the election campaign section of the course.

International Issues

In the world issues section you should also study the possible motivations of international organisations in their attempts to resolve issues/conflicts. The international agencies explored are:

- The United Nations Organisation
- Various NGOs
- The European Union
- regional organisations (e.g. the African Union, NATO).

So you are now ready to answer the exam questions.

Good luck!

Remember that the rewards for passing National 5 Modern Studies are well worth it! Your pass will help you get the future you want for yourself. In the exam, be confident in your own ability. If you're not sure how to answer a question, trust your instincts and just give it a go anyway. Keep calm and don't panic! GOOD LUCK!

NATIONAL 5

2014

National Qualifications 2014

X749/75/01

Modern Studies

TUESDAY, 29 APRIL
9:00 AM – 10:30 AM

Total marks — 60

SECTION 1 — DEMOCRACY IN SCOTLAND AND THE UNITED KINGDOM — 20 marks

Attempt ONE part, EITHER

SECTION 2 — SOCIAL ISSUES IN THE UNITED KINGDOM — 20 marks

Attempt ONE part, EITHER

SECTION 3 — INTERNATIONAL ISSUES — 20 marks

Attempt ONE part, EITHER

Write your answers clearly in the answer booklet provided. In the answer booklet you must clearly identify the question number you are attempting.

Use **blue** or **black** ink.

Before leaving the examination room you must give your answer booklet to the Invigilator; if you do not, you may lose all the marks for this paper.

[BLANK PAGE]

DO NOT WRITE ON THIS PAGE

SECTION 1 — DEMOCRACY IN SCOTLAND AND THE UNITED KINGDOM — 20 marks

Attempt ONE part, either

Part A — Democracy in Scotland   on pages 3–5

OR

Part B — Democracy in the United Kingdom   on pages 7–9

PART A — DEMOCRACY IN SCOTLAND

In your answers to Questions 1 and 2 you should give recent examples from Scotland.

Question 1

The Scottish Parliament has many devolved powers.

Describe, **in detail**, the devolved powers of the Scottish Parliament.   **6**

Question 2

Many people in Scotland choose to vote in elections.

Explain, **in detail**, why many people in Scotland choose to vote in elections.   **6**

[Turn over

PART A (continued)

Question 3

Study Sources 1, 2 and 3 then attempt the question which follows.

SOURCE 1

Scottish Parliament Election Factfile

Political parties have to keep detailed accounts of how much money they both receive and spend during elections. Political parties get their funding from a range of sources.

The Labour Party received approximately 36% of its donations at the 2011 election from the trade unions, whilst both the Conservatives and the SNP rely more on wealthy Scottish business people.

During the 2011 Scottish Parliament elections over £6·2 million was spent by the main political parties. This was however a drop from the £9·5 million spent in 2007.

A report on the 2011 Scottish Parliament election showed that most money was spent on campaign leaflets and letters from candidates. In 2007, the parties spent £1·2 million on these. In 2011, they spent £1·4 million.

In 2007, spending on advertising—such as billboards—was just over £1 million and £155,000 was spent on rallies and public meetings. In 2011, spending on advertising—such as billboards—was just over £438,600 and £47,000 was spent on rallies and public meetings.

In 2007, 22% of the public felt that there should be a ban on TV election broadcasts during elections. By 2011, this figure had fallen to 18%.

Voter awareness (%) of election campaign methods

Election	Received Leaflets	Noticed Billboard Advert	Attended a political meeting	Watched TV Broadcast
2007	89	62	3	70
2011	93	48	2	72

SOURCE 2

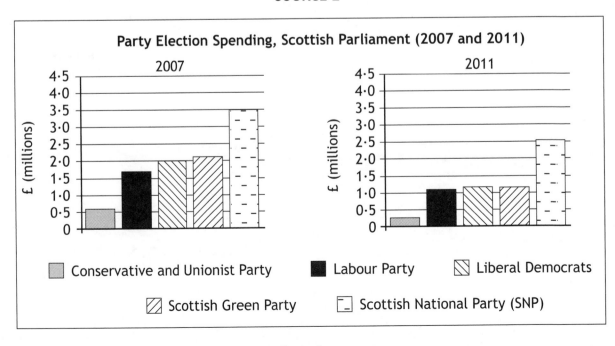

Party Election Spending, Scottish Parliament (2007 and 2011)

PART A Question 3 (continued)

SOURCE 3

Scottish Parliament Election Results (number of MSPs)

	Conservative	Labour	Liberal Democrats	SNP
2007	17	46	16	47
2011	15	37	5	69

The source of donations to all political parties (2011)

Other 15%

Company 15%

Individual 41%

Trade Union 29%

Using Sources 1, 2 and 3 what **conclusions** can be drawn about recent Scottish Parliament elections?

You should reach a conclusion about **each** of the following.

- The importance of trade union donations to the party election campaigns.
- The link between a party's election spending and election success.
- The link between election spending and voter awareness of election campaign methods.

Your conclusions **must** be supported by evidence from the sources. You should link information within and between the sources in support of your conclusions.

Your answer **must** be based on all three sources.

8

NOW GO TO SECTION 2 ON *PAGE ELEVEN*

[BLANK PAGE]

DO NOT WRITE ON THIS PAGE

PART B — DEMOCRACY IN THE UNITED KINGDOM

In your answers to Questions 1 and 2 you should give recent examples from the United Kingdom.

Question 1

> The UK Parliament has many reserved powers in Scotland.

Describe, **in detail**, the reserved powers of the UK Parliament in Scotland. 6

Question 2

> Many people in the UK choose to vote in elections.

Explain, **in detail**, why many people in the UK choose to vote in elections. 6

[Turn over

PART B (continued)

Question 3

Study Sources 1, 2 and 3 then attempt the question which follows.

SOURCE 1

UK General Election Factfile

Political parties have to keep detailed accounts of how much money they both receive and spend during elections. Political parties get their funding from a range of sources.

During the 2010 UK General Election ten parties reported receiving donations and loans totalling over £14 million. Many small parties however did not receive any money. The Labour Party received approximately 36% of its donations from trade unions in 2009 whilst the Conservatives and the Liberal Democrats relied more on donations from rich business individuals.

A report on the 2010 UK General Election showed that most money was spent on campaign leaflets and other materials such as letters from candidates. In 2005, the parties spent £8·9 million on these. In 2010, they spent £12·3 million.

In 2010, spending on advertising — such as billboards — was £9 million and £1·7 million was spent on rallies and public meetings. In 2005, spending on advertising — such as billboards — was £15 million and £4·1 million was spent on rallies and public meetings.

In 2005, 22% of the public felt that there should be a ban on TV election broadcasts during general elections. By 2010, this figure had fallen to 18%.

UK public's awareness (%) of election campaigns

Election	Received Leaflets (%)	Noticed Billboard Advert (%)	Attended a political meeting (%)	Watched TV Broadcast (%)
2005	89	62	4	70
2010	93	48	2	72

SOURCE 2

UK Political Party Spending in 2005 and 2010

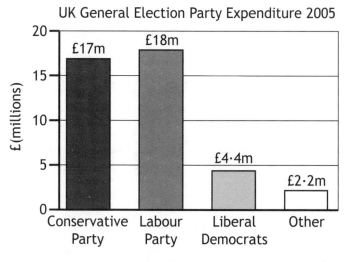

UK General Election Party Expenditure 2005

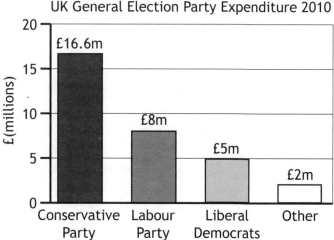

UK General Election Party Expenditure 2010

PART B Question 3 (continued)

SOURCE 3

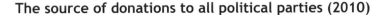

UK General Election Results (number of MPs)

	Conservative	Labour	Liberal Democrats	Others
2010	307	258	57	28
2005	198	356	62	30
2001	166	413	52	28

The source of donations to all political parties (2010)

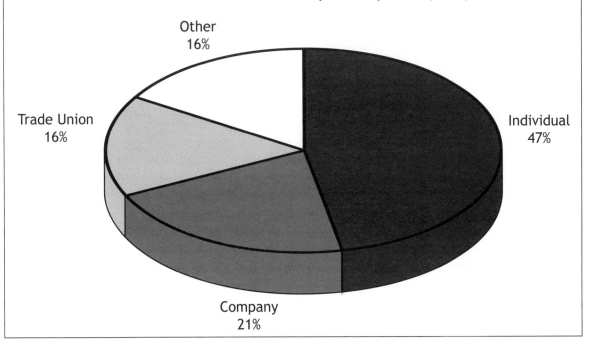

Using Sources 1, 2 and 3 what **conclusions** can be drawn about recent UK general elections?

You should reach a conclusion about **each** of the following.

- The importance of trade union donations to the party election campaigns.

- The link between a party's election spending and election success.

- The link between election spending and voter awareness of election campaign methods.

Your conclusions **must** be supported by evidence from the sources. You should link information within and between the sources in support of your conclusions.

Your answer **must** be based on all three sources.

8

NOW GO TO SECTION 2 ON *PAGE ELEVEN*

[BLANK PAGE]

DO NOT WRITE ON THIS PAGE

SECTION 2 — SOCIAL ISSUES IN THE UNITED KINGDOM — 20 marks

Attempt ONE part, either

Part C — Social Inequality   on pages 11–13

OR

Part D — Crime and the Law   on pages 15–17

PART C — SOCIAL INEQUALITY

In your answers to Questions 1 and 2 you should give recent examples from the United Kingdom.

Question 1

Groups that tackle inequality in the UK			
Government	Individuals	Voluntary sector	Private sector

Choose **one** of the groups above.

Describe, **in detail, two** ways in which the group you have chosen has tried to tackle inequality in the UK.   4

Question 2

Some people in the UK live in poverty, while others do not.

Explain, **in detail**, why some people in the UK live in poverty.   8

[Turn over

PART C (continued)

Question 3

Study Sources 1, 2 and 3 then attempt the question which follows.

SOURCE 1

The Daily Times

We May Be Fat But We're Healthier Than Ever

People in the UK are living longer than ever before despite concerns about health problems such as smoking and obesity (being significantly overweight). Average life expectancy in 2003 was 77 years. In 2013, it was 80 years. However the UK's life expectancy still compares poorly with other European countries.

Life expectancy in the UK has increased because we are making better lifestyle choices about our health, such as eating healthier food and exercising more. Life expectancy in the UK has also increased because of the good work of the NHS such as improvements in treating heart disease and cancers and Government policies such as anti-smoking laws. This has helped the UK reduce death rates from heart disease more than any other European country.

Many doctors warn that more has to be done to tackle the growing problem of childhood obesity and the health problems it causes. Since 2004, the number of obese children suffering from diabetes has doubled. If studies are accurate half of all adults in the UK will be obese by 2030.

SOURCE 2

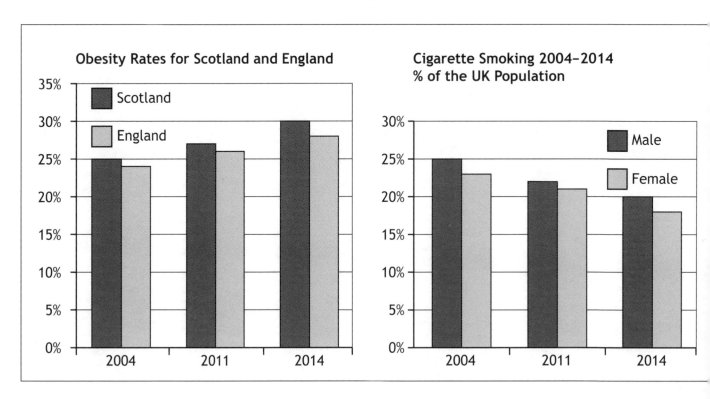

PART C Question 3 (continued)

SOURCE 3

Government Action to Reduce Smoking

The Government has worked hard to tackle the health problems associated with the issue of smoking. The Scottish Government banned smoking in public places in 2006. Since then the number of adults smoking has fallen, leading to a reduction in smoking related illness. England's smoke free laws came into effect one year later.

One study has found that the number of hospital admissions for children with asthma has gone from 26,969 cases in 2006 to 20,167 cases in 2013. Likewise, the number of hospital admissions for heart attacks linked to smoking has decreased.

Despite these improvements, one in five adults continues to smoke even though they know it is bad for their health. The highest rates of smoking in the UK are in Scotland with 27% of the adult population continuing to smoke. Smoking rates are also much higher within deprived inner city areas where rates have remained at 40% for the last 10 years.

Using Sources 1, 2 and 3, explain why the view of Sophie Wilson **is selective in the use of facts.**

> **There have been great improvements in the UK's health in the last 10 years.**
>
> **View of Sophie Wilson**

In your answer you **must:**

- give evidence from the sources that supports Sophie Wilson's view

and

- give evidence from the sources that opposes Sophie Wilson's view.

Your answer **must** be based on all three sources.

8

NOW GO TO SECTION 3 ON *PAGE NINETEEN*

[BLANK PAGE]

DO NOT WRITE ON THIS PAGE

PART D — CRIME AND THE LAW

In your answers to Questions 1 and 2 you should give recent examples from the United Kingdom.

Question 1

> The Children's Hearing System can help young people in Scotland in different ways.

Describe, **in detail, two** ways that the Children's Hearing System can help young people in Scotland.

4

Question 2

> Other punishments are increasingly being used as alternatives to prison sentences in the UK.

Explain, **in detail**, why other punishments are being used as alternatives to prison sentences in the UK.

8

[Turn over

PART D (continued)

Question 3

Study Sources 1, 2 and 3 then attempt the question which follows.

SOURCE 1

Facts and Viewpoints

The Victims and Witnesses (Scotland) Bill was introduced in 2013 by the Scottish Government and was intended to make sure that all victims and witnesses are guaranteed certain rights by law.

- The Victims and Witnesses Bill, proposes a "victim surcharge", meaning that those who commit crimes will contribute to the cost of providing support to victims eg house alarm systems and travel costs to hospital.

- Victim Support Scotland (VSS) is a voluntary group which provides a listening service for victims. Their volunteers can be easily contacted by phone, email or face to face.

- Victim Support volunteers are not trained counsellors and can only give practical information.

- Over £5 million per year is provided by the Scottish Government to support VSS and it has committed to maintaining that level of funding.

- Surveys show that victims are satisfied with the help and support given to them as victims of crime.

- The VSS run the Scottish Victim Crisis Centre (SVCC) but funding is so low that victims often get an engaged tone or an answering machine.

- The SVCC has a 9 month waiting list for victims who wish to talk about their experiences of crime.

- The Scottish Government give the SVCC £50,000 a year but staff say this is nowhere near enough to meet the demand for their services.

SOURCE 2

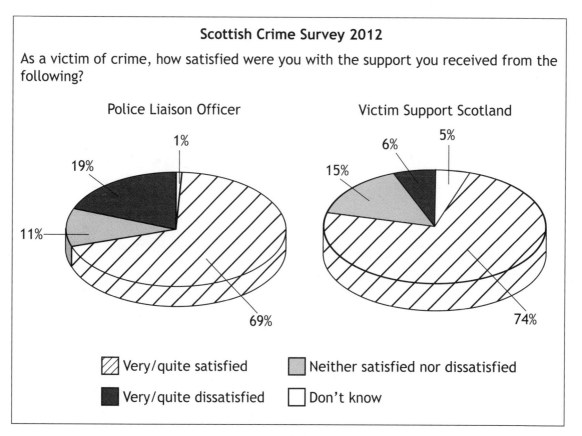

Scottish Crime Survey 2012

As a victim of crime, how satisfied were you with the support you received from the following?

Police Liaison Officer

1%
19%
11%
69%

Victim Support Scotland

5%
6%
15%
74%

- ▨ Very/quite satisfied
- ■ Very/quite dissatisfied
- ▦ Neither satisfied nor dissatisfied
- ☐ Don't know

PART D Question 3 (continued)

SOURCE 3

Statement by a Victim Support Campaigner

The Scottish Government has made a very positive attempt to support victims of crime in introducing the Victim and Witness Bill. They have clearly listened to what victims want and have introduced the victim surcharge which financially supports victims of crime. Victims on the whole are happy with the support they get from voluntary groups and the police. However, the funding given to some voluntary groups is simply not enough to support the level of demand for services such as counselling and advice. Some voluntary groups are not able to give full training to their staff as they can't afford it.

Using Sources 1, 2 and 3 explain why the view of Oliver Thomson **is selective in the use of facts**.

Victims of crime in Scotland receive satisfactory support.

View of Oliver Thomson

In your answer you **must**:

- give evidence from the sources that supports Oliver Thomson's view

and

- give evidence from the sources that opposes Oliver Thomson's view.

Your answer **must** be based on all three sources.   8

NOW GO TO SECTION 3 ON *PAGE NINETEEN*

[BLANK PAGE]

DO NOT WRITE ON THIS PAGE

SECTION 3 — INTERNATIONAL ISSUES — 20 marks

Attempt ONE part, either

Part E — World Powers   on pages 19–21

OR

Part F — World Issues   on pages 23–25

PART E — WORLD POWERS

In your answers to Questions 1 and 2 you should give recent examples from a world power you have studied.

Question 1

> Governments have made many attempts to tackle social and economic inequality.

Describe, **in detail**, **two** ways in which the government of the world power you have studied has tried to tackle social and economic inequality.   4

Question 2

> Some groups of people are more likely to participate in politics than others.

Explain, **in detail**, why some groups of people in the world power you have studied are more likely to participate in politics than others.   6

[Turn over

PART E (continued)

Question 3

Study Sources 1, 2 and 3 then attempt the question which follows.

You are a government adviser. You have been asked to recommend **whether or not** the Government of Australia should abolish compulsory voting.

Option 1	Option 2
Keep compulsory voting in Australia	Get rid of compulsory voting in Australia

SOURCE 1

Compulsory Voting

Most democratic governments consider voting in elections to be a right for all their citizens.

In Australia the government go further and punish those who do not vote with a fine. Voting in Australian elections is compulsory by law.

Australia has had some form of compulsory voting since the early 1900s and it is widely supported by Australian people. If you do not vote, you are fined $20 as punishment. You can be excused from voting if you provide a "valid and sufficient" reason eg serious illness.

Voter turnout in Australia was 47% prior to the 1924 compulsory voting law. In the decades since 1924, voter turnout has hovered around 95%.

In Australia 84% of people say they take voting seriously. However, 37% think a fine for not voting is fair. 9% of Australians admit to having at some time registered an informal vote (deliberately spoiling their paper).

Some suggest that it is undemocratic to force people to vote as it is against their right to freedom of choice. Opponents of compulsory voting argue that people with little interest in politics are forced to the polls; this increases the number of "informal votes". In addition, millions of dollars are spent on checking up on those who didn't turn out to vote.

SOURCE 2

Recent Election Statistics From Selected G20 Countries			
		Turnout (%)	Informal votes (%)
Countries **with** compulsory voting	Argentina	79·39	4·48
	Australia	93·22	5·6
	Brazil	81·88	8·64
Countries **without** compulsory voting	Canada	61·41	0·7
	Germany	70·78	1·44
	Russia	60·10	1·57

PART E Question 3 (continued)

SOURCE 3

Aussie News online: Compulsory voting could be scrapped

There is a possibility that nearly a century of compulsory voting will come to an end. Some politicians have recommended that it should be abolished. The Prime Minister of Australia wants to keep compulsory voting, despite calls to reform the election rules.

In the state of Queensland alone, about 250,000 people — roughly 8% of the roll — failed to vote in the last state election. Almost $1 million in state funds has been allocated to chase up those who failed to vote.

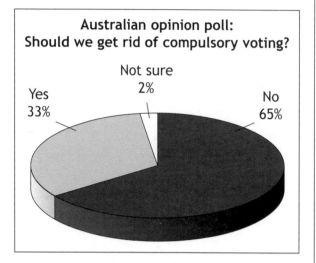

Australian opinion poll: Should we get rid of compulsory voting?

Not sure 2%
Yes 33%
No 65%

Have Your Say

Nic-C from Wilsonton   4 days ago

Forcing Australian citizens to vote is wrong. Everyone should have the right not to vote.

Ray Sunshine from Camp Hill   5 days ago

It's a privilege to vote. Compared to other countries, turnout here is much better so the results are more accurate.

Bruce T from Toowoomba South   5 days ago

People need to vote and not be lazy, but poor people don't have a way to get to their voting place unlike rich people who have cars.

Eileen Smith from Darling Heights   1 week ago

Forcing the population to vote means they will just deliberately spoil their ballot papers to avoid a fine.

Eddie from Ipswich   2 weeks ago

People who aren't interested should not be required to vote — bad decisions in the voting booth contribute to bad government.

Iain Thorpe from Mentone   2 months ago

When the turnout is low it means that a minority of society decide who the government is. I agree with most Australians who think we should keep compulsory voting.

You **must** decide which option to recommend, **either** keep compulsory voting in Australia (Option 1) **or** get rid of compulsory voting in Australia (Option 2).

    (i)   Using Sources 1, 2 and 3 **which option would you choose**?

    (ii)   Give reasons to **support** your choice.

    (iii)   **Explain** why you did not choose the other option.

Your answer **must** be based on all three sources.   **10**

[Turn over

[BLANK PAGE]

DO NOT WRITE ON THIS PAGE

PART F — WORLD ISSUES

In your answers to Questions 1 and 2 you should give recent examples from a world issue you have studied.

Question 1

> International organisations often try to resolve conflicts or issues without using military force.

Describe, **in detail**, **two** ways in which international organisations have tried to resolve a conflict **or** issue without using military force.   4

Question 2

> There are many factors which cause international conflicts and issues.

Explain, **in detail**, the factors which caused an international conflict **or** issue you have studied.   6

[Turn over

PART F (continued)

Question 3

Study Sources 1, 2 and 3 then attempt the question which follows.

You are a military adviser working for the North Atlantic Treaty Organisation (NATO) which is a military alliance. This is made up of the USA, UK and twenty six other Western countries.

You have been asked to recommend **whether or not** NATO should send in troops to stop the civil war in Country A.

Option 1: Send NATO troops to Country A	Option 2: Do not send NATO troops to Country A

SOURCE 1

Country A — Conflict in the Middle East

The conflict in Country A began as a series of huge anti-government demonstrations in early 2011. These protests became increasingly violent. Many hundreds of protestors were arrested, beaten, tortured and killed.

Country A's President had never tolerated any criticism of his Government by the people and free elections were never held. The media was also completely controlled by the President. Most of the people believe that democratic reform, fair elections and a free media are needed in Country A.

Protests soon escalated into a full-scale civil war. The rebel army announced its formation in July 2011 and mounted attacks on government targets. The United Nations estimate that so far, 140 000 people have been killed and that many of them were civilians, killed by the President's troops.

The rebel army had some success against the President's troops. Many Western governments gave the rebels weapons, equipment and money. The UK and the USA especially wanted to replace the President with a much friendlier government.

Many in the rebel army have been calling for the West to send in troops to help them defeat the "tyrant" President. Feelings are running high after reports that his Government troops used chemical weapons to kill over 600 civilians in an area controlled by the rebel army. However, many observers think that more armed troops would only make matters worse.

SOURCE 2

Public opinion poll
(Conducted in all 28 NATO countries — 10 000 citizens)

How strongly do you **agree or disagree** with the following statements?

	Strongly disagree (%)	Disagree (%)	Agree (%)	Strongly agree (%)
NATO should send troops to Country A	54	18	16	12
NATO cannot afford to send troops to Country A	12	19	27	42
More armed foreigners will make things worse	8	21	29	42
NATO troops wouldn't help the refugees	6	11	30	53
NATO must do everything to stop chemical weapons	6	9	35	50
NATO needs friendly Middle Eastern governments	15	26	20	39

PART F Question 3 (continued)

SOURCE 3

NATO News online: Troops in Country A?

NATO members are considering sending almost 100,000 troops to try to stop the fighting in Country A. This would be a huge step for NATO. Although NATO did use air power to help overthrow Gaddafi in Libya in 2011, this would be the first time NATO ground troops have ever been used outside Europe. The loss of life among NATO forces could be extremely high. Many NATO governments are very worried about the massive cost of such an operation.

Have Your Say

George-M from London   **6 hours ago**

The intervention in Libya cost the UK and USA 21·5 billion dollars and that didn't involve ground troops!

David-W from New York   **12 hours ago**

We cannot stand by and watch this President kill his own people with chemical weapons. NATO got rid of Gaddafi in Libya.

Katriona-N from Berlin   **yesterday**

Sending more foreigners with guns into Country A will just make things worse. There are enough men with guns already.

Karen-F from Madrid   **3 days ago**

Almost two million refugees have fled the country and are living in terrible conditions in stinking refugee camps. Neighbouring countries cannot cope any longer.

Andy-N from Rome   **last week**

The people of Country A have been lied to for too long by the President. Democracy is what they need.

Vikki-D from Liverpool   **last month**

Refugees desperately need help, not guns and bombs. Our governments mustn't sacrifice any more of our young soldiers.

You **must** decide which option to recommend, **either** send NATO troops to Country A (Option 1) **or** do not send NATO troops to Country A (Option 2).

    (i) Using Sources 1, 2 and 3 **which option would you choose**?

    (ii) Give reasons to **support** your choice.

    (iii) **Explain** why you did not choose the other option.

Your answer **must** be based on all three sources.   **10**

[END OF QUESTION PAPER]

Page twenty-five

[BLANK PAGE]

DO NOT WRITE ON THIS PAGE

National Qualifications 2015

X749/75/11

Modern Studies

WEDNESDAY, 27 MAY

9:00 AM – 10:45 AM

Total marks — 60

SECTION 1 — DEMOCRACY IN SCOTLAND AND THE UNITED KINGDOM — 20 marks

Attempt ONE part, EITHER

SECTION 2 — SOCIAL ISSUES IN THE UNITED KINGDOM — 20 marks

Attempt ONE part, EITHER

SECTION 3 — INTERNATIONAL ISSUES — 20 marks

Attempt ONE part, EITHER

Write your answers clearly in the answer booklet provided. In the answer booklet you must clearly identify the question number you are attempting.

Use **blue** or **black** ink.

Before leaving the examination room you must give your answer booklet to the Invigilator; if you do not, you may lose all the marks for this paper.

MARKS

SECTION 1 — DEMOCRACY IN SCOTLAND AND THE UNITED KINGDOM — 20 marks

Attempt ONE part, either

Part A — Democracy in Scotland   on pages 2–5

OR

Part B — Democracy in the United Kingdom   on pages 6–9

PART A — DEMOCRACY IN SCOTLAND

In your answers to Questions 1 and 2 you should give recent examples from Scotland.

Question 1

> Local councils provide many services in Scotland.

Describe, **in detail**, **two** services provided by local councils in Scotland.   4

Question 2

> People in Scotland can participate in society in many ways.

Explain, **in detail**, why some people participate in **one** of the following:

- Pressure Groups
- Trade Unions
- The Media.   6

[Turn over for Question 3 on *Page four*]

DO NOT WRITE ON THIS PAGE

PART A (continued)

Question 3

Study Sources 1, 2 and 3 and then answer the question which follows.

Glenlochy is about to elect a new MSP. You are a voter in Glenlochy. You are undecided between Option 1 and Option 2.

Using sources 1, 2 and 3 you must decide which option to choose.

Option 1 Daisy Frost, candidate for the Scottish Labour Party	**Option 2** Tom Kirk, candidate for the Scottish National Party

SOURCE 1

BestPals   🏠 Home   ⚙ Settings   ▼   Search 🔍

Daisy Frost

Age 56

Studied Politics at Abertay University

Currently a local councillor

If I am elected to represent Glenlochy I will work to ensure that more women are elected to the Scottish Parliament. I believe that the lack of women in Holyrood has affected the number of women working locally. This needs to change.

Unemployment is clearly a problem in the local area and I would work hard to increase job opportunities. A lack of internet access is an obvious barrier and I would seek to improve this.

Crime is not a major concern so I would not focus on this if elected but would try to increase access to childcare as this is important to the community. Health care is an area I am passionate about and health in Glenlochy needs to improve. The lives of the people of Glenlochy are being cruelly cut short and I pledge to change this.

Tom Kirk

Age 35

Studied Law at Aberdeen University

Currently a lawyer for Citizens' Advice

Employment is a key area which I will try to improve if elected. Too few local people are in full-time work. This means that too many are also relying on benefits to get by.

I will work hard to ensure that the elderly of Glenlochy continue to be treated with dignity and feel safe in the local community. The majority of local people agree with me that elderly people are well cared for.

Skills education is key to any improvements in Glenlochy. Unfortunately at the moment too many local children are leaving school before S6 without the skills they need.

Childcare is not a major concern so I would not focus on this if elected but would try to decrease crime as this is a major concern in the community.

PART A Question 3 (continued)   MARKS

SOURCE 2

Selected Facts about Glenlochy

Glenlochy is a constituency for the Scottish Parliament in central Scotland. This part of Scotland used to rely on coal mining as its main industry. There is now only one major employer, a call centre in the main town of Glenlochy. Last month it made 100 full-time workers redundant. Parts of the area are amongst the most deprived in Scotland and there are few job opportunities. Average life expectancy in the area is 77 compared to a Scottish average of 79.

Glenlochy Constituency is holding a by-election due to the death of the previous MSP. Many people feel the area now needs an experienced representative.

There was a local meeting about crime levels last month in the town hall where 530 residents turned up to speak to the local community police officer about their concerns. Carol Fife, Chair of the Community Council said "Crime is clearly increasing. We are very worried about this issue. Our new MSP needs to have a legal background".

Opinion Poll of 1000 Glenlochy Residents

	The elderly are well looked after in Glenlochy	Crime is a problem in Glenlochy	The Scottish Parliament needs more female MSPs	A lack of childcare is a major problem locally
Strongly agree	12%	30%	21%	36%
Agree	23%	35%	33%	32%
Disagree	25%	26%	25%	22%
Strongly disagree	40%	9%	21%	10%

SOURCE 3

Glenlochy Statistics (%)

	Glenlochy	Scotland
Unemployed and seeking work	9	7
Claiming benefits	17·5	15·8
Full-time employment	42	48
Women in work	34	45
Suffering long-term ill health	15	18
Pupils completing S6 at school	56	54
Households with internet access	79	76

You must decide which option to recommend, **either** Daisy Frost (**Option 1**) **or** Tom Kirk (**Option 2**).

(i)   Using Sources 1, 2 and 3, **which option would you choose?**

(ii)   Give reasons to **support** your choice.

(iii)   **Explain** why you did not choose the other option.

Your answer **must** be based on all three sources.   10

NOW GO TO SECTION 2 ON *PAGE TEN*

MARK.

PART B — DEMOCRACY IN THE UNITED KINGDOM

In your answers to Questions 4 and 5 you should give recent examples from the United Kingdom.

Question 4

> The House of Lords has an important role in the UK Government.

Describe, **in detail**, **two** of the roles the House of Lords has in the UK Government.   **4**

Question 5

> People in the UK can participate in society in many ways.

Explain, **in detail**, why some people participate in **one** of the following:

- Pressure Groups
- Trade Unions
- The Media.   **6**

[Turn over for Question 6 on *Page eight*]

DO NOT WRITE ON THIS PAGE

PART B (continued)

Question 6

Study Sources 1, 2 and 3 and then answer the question which follows.

Millwood is about to elect a new MP. You are a voter in Millwood. You are undecided between Option 1 and Option 2

Using sources 1, 2 and 3 you must decide which option to choose.

Option 1	**Option 2**
Nora Manson, candidate for the Scottish Conservative Party	John Donaldson, candidate for the Scottish Liberal Democratic Party

SOURCE 1

BestPals   🏠 Home   ⚙ Settings   ▼ Search   🔍

Nora Manson
Age 56
Studied Politics at Glasgow University
Currently a local councillor
Born in Millwood

John Donaldson
Age 35
Studied Law at Edinburgh University
Currently a lawyer for Citizens' Advice
Born in Millwood

If I am elected to represent Millwood I will work to ensure that more women are elected to the UK parliament. I believe that the lack of women in Westminster has an effect on the number of women working locally. This needs to change.

Unemployment is clearly a problem in the local area and I would work hard to increase job opportunities. A lack of internet access is an obvious barrier and I would seek to improve this.

Crime is not a major concern so I would not focus on this if elected but would try to increase access to childcare as this is important to the community. Health care is an area I am passionate about and health in Millwood needs to improve. The lives of the people of Millwood are being cruelly cut short and I pledge to change this.

Employment is a key area which I will try to improve if elected. Too few local people are in full-time work. This means that too many are also relying on benefits to get by.

I will work hard to ensure that the elderly of Millwood are treated with dignity and feel safe in the local community. The majority of local people agree with me that elderly people are well cared for.

Skills education is vital if improvements are to be made. At the moment too many local children are leaving school before S6 without the skills they need.

Childcare is not a major concern so I would not focus on this if elected, but would try to decrease crime as this is a major concern in the community.

PART B Question 6 (continued)   MARKS

SOURCE 2

Selected Facts about Millwood

Millwood is a constituency for the UK Parliament in central Scotland. This part of Scotland used to rely on steelmaking as its main industry. There is now only one major employer, a call centre in the main town of Millwood. Last month it made 100 full-time workers redundant. Parts of the area are amongst the most deprived in the UK and there are few job opportunities. Average life expectancy in the area is 77 compared to a UK average of 80.

Millwood Constituency is holding a by-election due to the death of the previous MP. Many people feel the area now needs an experienced representative.

There was a local meeting about crime levels last month in the town hall where 530 residents turned up to speak to the local community police officer about their concerns. Lynn Morrow, Chair of the Community Council said "Crime is clearly increasing. We are very worried about this issue. Our new MP needs to have a legal background".

Opinion Poll of 1000 Millwood Residents

	The elderly are well looked after in Millwood	Crime is a problem in Millwood	The UK Parliament needs more female MPs	A lack of childcare is a major problem locally
Strongly agree	12%	26%	21%	36%
Agree	23%	35%	33%	32%
Disagree	25%	30%	25%	22%
Strongly disagree	40%	9%	21%	10%

SOURCE 3

Millwood Statistics (%)

	Millwood	UK
Unemployed and seeking work	9	6
Claiming benefits	17·5	15·2
Full-time employment	42	49
Women in work	34	45
Suffering long-term ill health	15	18
Pupils completing S6 at school	56	53
Households with internet access	79	77

You must decide which option to recommend, **either** Nora Manson (**Option 1**) **or** John Donaldson (**Option 2**).

(i)   Using Sources 1, 2 and 3, **which option would you choose**?

(ii)   Give reasons to **support** your choice.

(iii)   **Explain** why you did not choose the other option.

Your answer **must** be based on all three sources.   10

NOW GO TO SECTION 2 ON *PAGE TEN*

MARKS

SECTION 2 — SOCIAL ISSUES IN THE UNITED KINGDOM — 20 marks

Attempt ONE part, either

Part C — Social Inequality   on pages 10–13

OR

Part D — Crime and the Law   on pages 14–17

PART C — SOCIAL INEQUALITY

In your answers to Questions 7 and 8 you should give recent examples from the United Kingdom.

Question 7

> The UK Government tries to reduce social inequality.

Describe, **in detail**, **two** ways in which the UK Government tries to reduce social inequality.   **4**

Question 8

> There are many groups in the UK which experience inequality.

Explain, **in detail**, the reasons why one or more groups you have studied experiences inequality in the UK.   **8**

[Turn over for Question 9 on *Page twelve*]

DO NOT WRITE ON THIS PAGE

PART C (continued)

Question 9

Study Sources 1, 2 and 3 and then answer the question which follows.

SOURCE 1

Poverty Factfile (2013 – 2014)

There are still 3·6 million children living in poverty in the United Kingdom. This means that a quarter (25%) of children in the UK currently live in poverty.

According to the UK Government, an average family needs to have £349 each week to meet their basic needs. The reality of living in poverty means that many families have only about £12 per day, per person to cover the basic cost of living. Children living in poverty often go without the items many children take for granted such as a bike or going on a school trip.

Poverty also has a negative impact on the health of a child with poor children experiencing more ill health than richer children. In addition, 24% of the poorest families cannot afford to keep their house warm compared to just 3% of wealthy families.

The UK Government is trying to reduce the problem of poverty. It recently set the ambitious targets that no more than 4% of children will be living in absolute poverty with a target of 12% for relative poverty by the year 2020. Absolute poverty is when someone cannot afford the basic necessities of life eg food, shelter. Relative poverty is in comparison to average incomes within a country.

Living in poverty can reduce a child's expectation of their own life and can often lead to a lifetime of poverty. Many people believe that it is the government's responsibility to help children improve their life chances and escape the cycle of poverty.

SOURCE 2

Selected Family Statistics

	Children Living in the Poorest Families	Children Living in the Richest Families
Average life expectancy at birth (years)	71	82
Childhood obesity rates	25%	18%
Average weekly family spending on food	£49	£70
Families who cannot afford a week's holiday per year	62%	6%

Estimated Child Poverty Rates in the United Kingdom 2016 – 2022

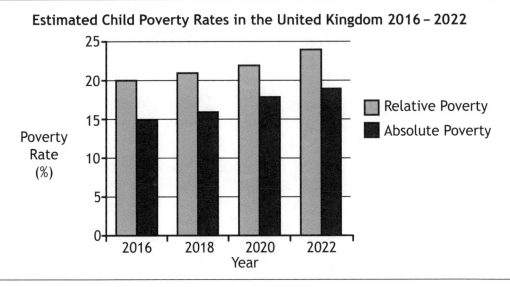

MARKS

PART C Question 9 (continued)

SOURCE 3

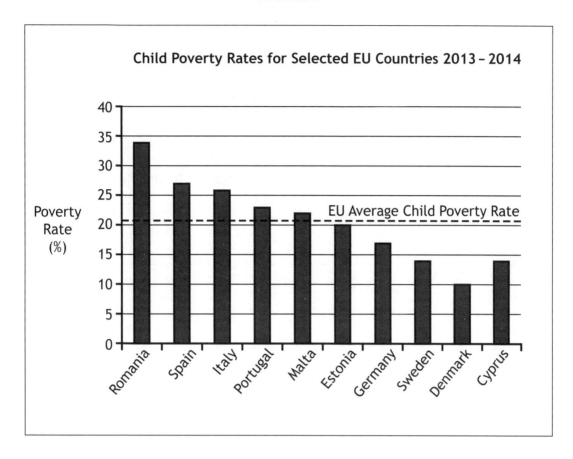

Using Sources 1, 2 and 3, what **conclusions** can be drawn about the issue of child poverty.

You should reach a conclusion about **each** of the following.

- The impact of poverty on a child's life

- The UK Government's progress towards meeting its targets for 2020

- UK child poverty rates compared to other countries

Your conclusions **must** be supported by evidence from the sources. You should link information within and between the sources in support of your conclusions.

Your answer **must** be based on all three sources.

8

NOW GO TO SECTION 3 ON *PAGE EIGHTEEN*

MARKS

PART D — CRIME AND THE LAW

In your answers to Questions 10 and 11 you should give recent examples from the United Kingdom.

Question 10

> Scottish courts have the power to punish people.

Describe, **in detail**, **two** different ways that Scottish Courts can punish people.

4

Question 11

> There are many factors which cause crime in the UK.

Explain, **in detail**, the factors which cause crime in the UK.

8

[Turn over for Question 12 on *Page sixteen*]

DO NOT WRITE ON THIS PAGE

PART D (continued)

Question 12

Study Sources 1, 2 and 3 below and then answer the question which follows.

SOURCE 1

Social Media and the Law

The law that has been used to prosecute people for sending inappropriate messages via social media is section 127 of the Communications Act 2003.

This states that a person is guilty of an offence if they send, post or forward a message online that is offensive or of an indecent, obscene or menacing character.

Social Media has become an important part of all areas of our daily lives. However, only one in five people (19%) read the terms and conditions of sites, and only one in ten know about social media laws, or have heard of the Communications Act 2003.

Communications sent via social media can be classed as criminal offences and companies now have more rules about the use of social media in their contracts and policies. A growing number of employers are now using social media sites to investigate people who have applied for a job. When surveyed, 63% of 16 to 18 year olds wrongly believed that this was against the law.

It is an offence to cause distress or threaten individuals online and those who embark on "trolling" can expect to be prosecuted by the police. Many people feel that they can behave differently online as they believe they are anonymous. However, more and more people are being prosecuted for their online activities and have received punishments from the courts.

Some police forces recognise that this is a very serious problem but they are extremely concerned that resources are being wasted — they estimate that two thirds of incidents reported to them are for petty online arguments.

SOURCE 2

Memo to Employees

GLENINCH COUNCIL

Dear Employees,

A recent University report suggests that the Scottish economy is losing millions of pounds because of workers using social media inappropriately during work time. Social media breaks are now costing us more than cigarette breaks!

Many of you will already be using social media in a variety of ways in your lives outside work. This memo will help you use social media responsibly at work.

We recognise the opportunities offered by social media and would like staff to use it to enhance the work of the Council.

However, you must respect the needs of the Council to protect its reputation.

If you use social media irresponsibly there is a risk that the Council will be damaged. We expect you to use social media responsibly and with care. If you do not do this you could be disciplined, face the sack or be prosecuted by the police. Sending inappropriate messages or taking social media breaks when you are supposed to be working will not be tolerated.

PART D Question 12 (continued)

SOURCE 3

Social Media Statistics

Opinion Poll

Question — Are you aware of the possible consequences of sending an offensive Tweet?

Yes	25%
No	75%

Social media – Complaints and prosecutions

	Complaints made to police about offensive posts on social media	Successful prosecutions
2010	2,347	60
2011	2,490	90
2012	2,563	107
2013	2,672	142
2014	2,703	240

Hours lost through social media breaks throughout the UK

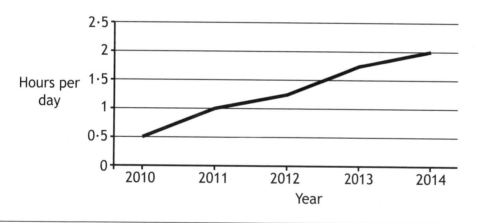

Using Sources 1, 2 and 3, what **conclusions** can be drawn about the law concerning social media.

You should reach a conclusion about each of the following:

- The level of public awareness of the law concerning social media
- Social media and the workplace
- Crime associated with social media.

Your conclusions must be supported by evidence from the sources. You should link information within and between the sources in support of your conclusions.

Your answer must be based on all three sources.

8

NOW GO TO SECTION 3 ON *PAGE EIGHTEEN*

MARKS

SECTION 3 — INTERNATIONAL ISSUES — 20 marks

Attempt ONE part, either

Part E — World Powers   on pages 18–21

OR

Part F — World Issues   on pages 22–25

PART E — WORLD POWERS

In your answers to Questions 13 and 14 you should give recent examples from a world power you have studied.

Question 13

> World Powers can have an impact on other countries.

Describe, **in detail**, **two ways** the World Power you have studied has had an impact on other countries.

In your answer you should state the world power you have studied.   **6**

Question 14

> In all World Powers, some groups of people are poorly represented in government.

Explain, **in detail**, why some groups of people are poorly represented in the government of the world power you have studied.

In your answer you should state the world power you have studied.   **6**

[Turn over for Question 15 on *Page twenty*]

DO NOT WRITE ON THIS PAGE

PART E (continued)

Question 15

Study Sources 1, 2 and 3 and then answer the question which follows.

Source 1

Gun Ownership in Selected G20 Countries

 USA — Guns : *ALLOWED*

According to the US Constitution all Americans can own a gun. A US Government report found that gun ownership increased from 192 million firearms in 1994 to 310 million firearms in 2009, but levels of crime fell sharply. Gun control campaigners argue that the easy availability of guns increases crime. The Brady Campaign to Prevent Gun Violence found that the US firearm homicide rate is 20 times higher than the combined rates of 22 countries with similar levels of wealth. A study from Harvard University said "there is no evidence which proves widespread gun ownership among the general population leads to higher incidents of murder."

FRANCE — Guns: *ALLOWED* **JAPAN — Guns: *BANNED***

Rules around gun ownership are strict eg you must see a doctor every year to get a certificate to prove you are physically and mentally able.	The weapons law begins by stating "No-one shall possess a firearm or firearms or a sword or swords", and very few exceptions are allowed.

BRAZIL — Guns: *ALLOWED*  **INDIA — Guns: *BANNED***

In 2004, the number of gun-related injuries was 36,000. Despite this, in a 2005 referendum, 65% of the Brazilian population voted against banning the sale of guns and ammunition.	The law prevents the sale, manufacture, possession, import, export and transport of firearms and ammunition.

 RUSSIA — Guns: *BANNED*

Ownership of most types of guns is illegal for Russian civilians. Despite this, public shootings still happen. In November 2012, 30-year-old lawyer Dmitry Vinogradov walked into the Moscow offices of a medical company where he worked, and opened fire on his colleagues — murdering six and critically injuring one more. Right to Bear Arms, a Moscow based pressure group which represents gun owners, claimed "We have conducted studies which identify a clear pattern: the more a society is armed, the lower the level of criminal violence."

Page twenty

PART E Question 15 (continued)

Source 2

More Guns = More Deaths?

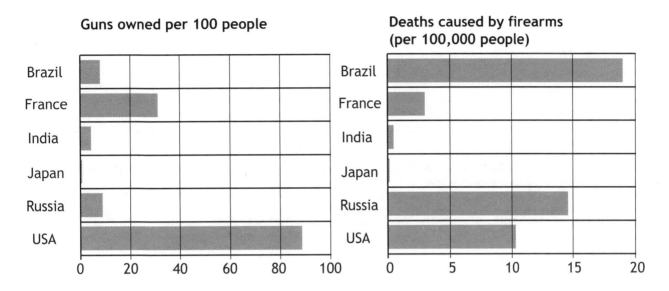

Guns owned per 100 people

Deaths caused by firearms (per 100,000 people)

SOURCE 3

Crime Statistics

Country	Murder Rate per 100,000	Violent Crime per 100,000	Robbery per 100,000
Brazil	27	504	110
France	1·65	201	100·8
India	1·5	162	1·6
Japan	0·4	98	4·0
Russia	10·2	584	90·3
USA	4·7	386	146·4

Using Sources 1, 2 and 3, explain why the view of **Kristen Nunez is selective in the use of facts.**

> Countries which allow gun ownership are safer places to live.
>
> View of Kristen Nunez

In your answer you must:

- give evidence from the sources that supports Kristen Nunez's view

and

- give evidence from the sources that opposes Kristen Nunez's view.

Your answer **must** be based on all three sources.   **8**

MARK

PART F — WORLD ISSUES

In your answers to Questions 16 and 17 you should give recent examples from a world issue you have studied.

Question 16

Ordinary people are often affected by international issues and conflicts.

Describe, **in detail**, **two** ways ordinary people have been affected by an international issue **or** conflict you have studied.

In your answer you should state the world issue or conflict you have studied.

6

Question 17

International Organisations attempt to resolve issues and conflicts.

Selected International Organisations		
United Nations	NATO	European Union
Charities	NGOs	African Union

Select an International Organisation you have studied.

Explain, in detail, the reasons why it has succeeded **or** failed in resolving an international issue **or** conflict.

In your answer you should state the world issue or conflict you have studied.

6

[Turn over for Question 18 on *Page twenty-four*]

DO NOT WRITE ON THIS PAGE

PART F (continued)

Question 18

Study Sources 1, 2 and 3 and then answer the question which follows.

Source 1

Illegal Drug Producers and Users

Drug producer: Afghanistan - Heroin and Marijuana

Afghanistan produces more opium than any other country in the world. Crops have dropped by 10% recently and the President recently stated that "Afghanistan is now a safer place to live." Almost all of the heroin used in Europe comes from Afghanistan's opium fields. In addition Afghanistan also supplies large amounts of marijuana to the world. Two aid workers travelling in Herat city were shot dead by an armed drug gang in July 2014.

Drug Producer: Peru - Cocaine and Heroin

Peru is the second largest producer of cocaine in the world. Until 1996, Peru was number one, but was then overtaken by Colombia.

Drug producer: Colombia - Cocaine

Colombia produces more cocaine than any other country in the world. They provide almost all of the cocaine consumed in the United States, as well as in other countries. Certain parts of the country are "no-go" areas for tourists and the police.

Drug user: The USA - Marijuana

Over 51% of all American adults have used marijuana at some stage in their lives. This is the highest figure in the world. Criminal gangs make billions of dollars and recently one gang member admitted to murdering forty enemies from other gangs. In a recent speech, President Obama stressed that the murder rate in the USA had halved in the last twenty years.

Drug user: Iran - Heroin

Iran has one of the highest rates of heroin use in the world. 2·3% of adults have used heroin in the last year.

Drug user: El Salvador - Cocaine

The small Central American country of El Salvador has a big issue with cocaine use. One in every forty people are regular users. Around 60 000 people are members of organised criminal gangs but the government has reduced the murder rate by 80% in recent years.

PART F Question 18 (continued)

Source 2

More Drugs = More Crime?

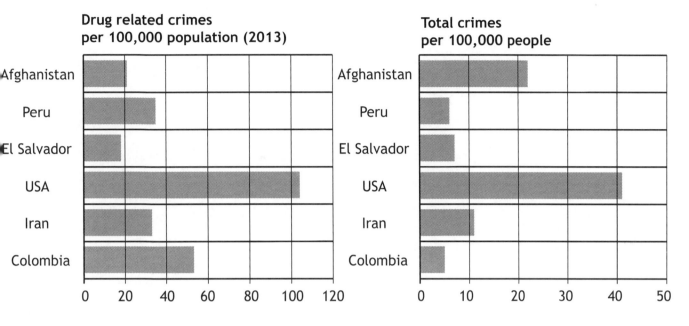

Drug related crimes per 100,000 population (2013)

Total crimes per 100,000 people

SOURCE 3

Crime Statistics

Country	Murder Rate per 100,000	Violent Kidnappings per 100,000	Serious Assaults per 100,000
Afghanistan	3·4	56	33
Peru	5·7	46	100
El Salvador	57·5	0·1	176
USA	4·7	17	874
Iran	3·9	4	44
Colombia	61·1	65	63

Using Sources 1, 2 and 3, explain why the view of **Ted King is selective in the use of facts**.

> Countries which produce illegal drugs are more dangerous places to live.
>
> View of Ted King

In your answer you must:

- give evidence from the sources that supports Ted King's view

and

- give evidence from the sources that opposes Ted King's view.

Your answer **must** be based on all three sources.

8

[END OF QUESTION PAPER]

Page twenty-five

[BLANK PAGE]

DO NOT WRITE ON THIS PAGE

NATIONAL 5

2016

National Qualifications 2016

X749/75/11

Modern Studies

MONDAY, 30 MAY

1:00 PM – 2:45 PM

Total marks — 60

SECTION 1 — DEMOCRACY IN SCOTLAND AND THE UNITED KINGDOM — 20 marks

Attempt ONE part, EITHER

Part A	Democracy in Scotland	Pages 2–5
OR		
Part B	Democracy in the United Kingdom	Pages 6–9

SECTION 2 — SOCIAL ISSUES IN THE UNITED KINGDOM — 20 marks

Attempt ONE part, EITHER

Part C	Social Inequality	Pages 10–13
OR		
Part D	Crime and the Law	Pages 14–17

SECTION 3 — INTERNATIONAL ISSUES — 20 marks

Attempt ONE part, EITHER

Part E	World Powers	Pages 18–21
OR		
Part F	World Issues	Pages 22–25

Write your answers clearly in the answer booklet provided. In the answer booklet you must clearly identify the question number you are attempting.

Use **blue** or **black** ink.

Before leaving the examination room you must give your answer booklet to the Invigilator; if you do not, you may lose all the marks for this paper.

MARKS

SECTION 1 — DEMOCRACY IN SCOTLAND AND THE UNITED KINGDOM — 20 marks

Attempt ONE part, either

Part A — Democracy in Scotland   on pages 2–5

OR

Part B — Democracy in the United Kingdom   on pages 6–9

PART A — DEMOCRACY IN SCOTLAND

In your answers to Questions 1 and 2 you should give recent examples from Scotland.

Question 1

> In Scottish Parliament Elections political parties campaign in many ways.

Describe, **in detail**, **two** ways political parties campaign in Scottish Parliament Elections.

4

Question 2

> The Additional Member System (AMS) has several advantages.

Explain, **in detail**, the advantages of the Additional Member System (AMS).

You should give a **maximum** of **three** advantages in your answer.

8

[Turn over for next question]

DO NOT WRITE ON THIS PAGE

PART A (continued)

Question 3

Study Sources 1, 2 and 3 and then answer the question which follows.

SOURCE 1

Extracts from a report on Scottish political attitudes

"People in Scotland have many opportunities to participate in politics, for example voting in local authority and European Parliament elections. There has been concern that fewer are taking part in the political process. Most people still see voting as important, but in the last three General Elections (2005, 2010, 2015) between 30% and 41% of the Scottish electorate didn't vote. Political parties are interested in finding out the reasons for this.

Younger voters have significantly lower turnout rates at elections than the middle-aged and elderly. Since 2001 no General Election has seen more than 50% of young people turn out to vote. Traditional forms of participation are less appealing to young people but they are taking part in politics in new ways, such as petitioning, boycotts, demonstrations and online activity such as blogging and internet campaigning.

Engagement in politics can be measured by looking at membership of the main political parties. The Green Party and the SNP have experienced increases in their membership over the last decade while the "traditional" parties (Conservative, Labour and Liberal Democrats) have seen a reduction in membership."

SOURCE 2

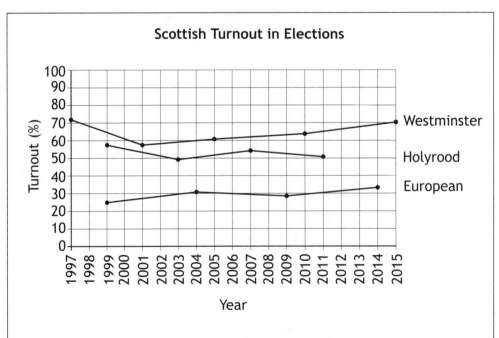

Scottish Turnout in Elections

% who have taken part in selected activities, by age

	18-29	30-59	60+
Signed petition	36%	34%	30%
Gone on a protest or demonstration	10%	7%	6%
Contacted radio, TV or newspaper	3%	5%	10%
Contacted your MP	5%	17%	20%

MARKS

PART A Question 3 (continued)

SOURCE 3

Turnout in the Scottish Independence Referendum (by selected Local Authority)

Dundee **78·8%**

Stirling **90·1%**

East Dunbartonshire **91%**

Glasgow **75%**

East Renfrewshire **90·4%**

Scotland Decides NO — **NO 55% YES 45%** Final Result

The Tribune
PARTY FIGURES
Party membership changed - SNP membership prior to the referendum was 26,000 and by April 2015 it was 105,000.

EVENING STAR
Referendum Discussion
65% of Scots say they had "lots of conversations with family and friends" about the referendum, compared with 29% who had not. 11% said that they had contributed to an online discussion and 9% had attended a public meeting. Social media was the most popular place for under-18's to turn to for information, with 64% using this.

the DAILY ALBA
SCOTTISH POWERS
In meeting the promise to grant more powers to Scotland after the referendum, far more people trust the SNP (37%) to Labour (15%), the Conservatives (8%) and the Liberal Democrats (1%) combined.

Using Sources 1, 2 and 3, explain why the view of Ross Monroe **is selective in the use of facts.**

> There are high levels of political participation in Scotland.
>
> View of Ross Monroe

In your answer you **must**:

- give evidence from the sources that supports Ross Monroe's view

and

- give evidence from the sources that opposes Ross Monroe's view.

Your answer **must** be based on all **three** sources.

8

NOW GO TO SECTION 2 ON *PAGE TEN*

MARK

PART B — DEMOCRACY IN THE UNITED KINGDOM

In your answers to Questions 4 and 5 you should give recent examples from the United Kingdom.

Question 4

> In General Elections political parties campaign in many ways.

Describe, **in detail**, **two** ways in which political parties campaign during General Elections.

4

Question 5

> First Past the Post has several disadvantages.

Explain, **in detail**, the disadvantages of First Past the Post.

You should give a **maximum** of **three** disadvantages in your answer.

8

[Turn over for next question]

DO NOT WRITE ON THIS PAGE

PART B (continued)

Question 6

Study Sources 1, 2 and 3 and then answer the question which follows.

SOURCE 1

Composition of the House of Lords

The House of Commons and the House of Lords make up the two Chambers in the UK Parliament. In recent years, some changes have been made to the composition of the Lords. In 1995, over half of those who sat in the House of Lords were hereditary peers (this means they inherited their seat in the Lords from their father). The total number of Lords has changed and currently there are about 790 members, none of whom are directly elected by the public.

By 1997, about 36% of the House of Lords were appointed as a Lord for the length of their life (a life peer). Today, approximately 90% of Lords are life peers. Many Lords bring great experience and expertise to Parliament in the fields of medicine, law, business, science, sport and education to name a few areas.

Although women have only been allowed to sit in the House of Lords since 1958, the Lords Speaker is currently a woman, Baroness D'Souza. It is her job to oversee the business in the House of Lords. She has a special interest in human rights and development issues. Since 2000, 36% of newly appointed members have been women, 21% have been ethnic minorities and 10% have been disabled.

SOURCE 2

Comparison of selected factors in the House of Lords and the UK population

	House of Lords		UK population	
	1995	**2015**	**1995**	**2015**
Male	93%	75%	49%	49%
Female	7%	25%	51%	51%
Ethnic-minority background	Less than 1%	5%	6%	13%
% under 60 years of age	22%	16%	81%	77%
Average age	79	70	36	40
Privately educated	62%	50%	7%	7%
Graduated from Oxford or Cambridge University	35%	38%	Less than 1%	Less than 1%
Disabled	2%	11%	12%	17%

PART B Question 6 (continued)

MARKS

SOURCE 3

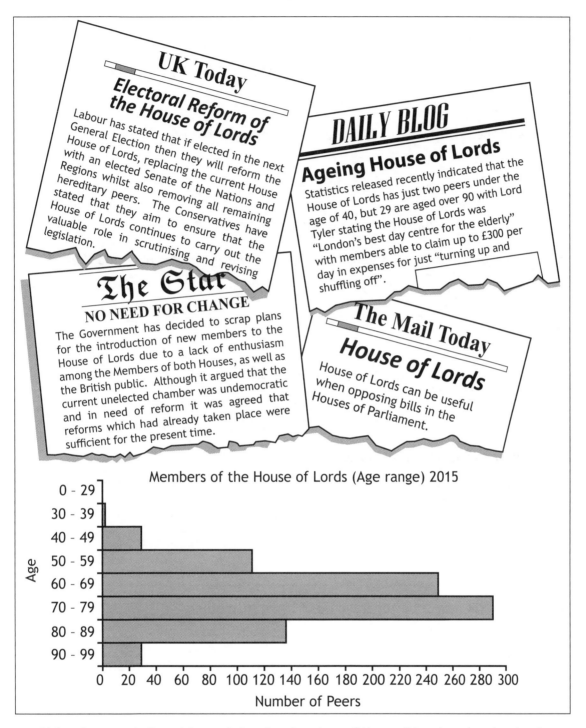

UK Today

Electoral Reform of the House of Lords

Labour has stated that if elected in the next General Election then they will reform the House of Lords, replacing the current House with an elected Senate of the Nations and Regions whilst also removing all remaining hereditary peers. The Conservatives have stated that they aim to ensure that the House of Lords continues to carry out the valuable role in scrutinising and revising legislation.

DAILY BLOG

Ageing House of Lords

Statistics released recently indicated that the House of Lords has just two peers under the age of 40, but 29 are aged over 90 with Lord Tyler stating the House of Lords was "London's best day centre for the elderly" with members able to claim up to £300 per day in expenses for just "turning up and shuffling off".

The Star

NO NEED FOR CHANGE

The Government has decided to scrap plans for the introduction of new members to the House of Lords due to a lack of enthusiasm among the Members of both Houses, as well as the British public. Although it argued that the current unelected chamber was undemocratic and in need of reform it was agreed that reforms which had already taken place were sufficient for the present time.

The Mail Today

House of Lords

House of Lords can be useful when opposing bills in the Houses of Parliament.

Members of the House of Lords (Age range) 2015

Using Sources 1, 2 and 3, explain why the view of Morag Watt **is selective in the use of facts.**

> The House of Lords is in need of further reform.
>
> View of Morag Watt

In your answer you **must:**

- give evidence from the sources that supports Morag Watt's view

and

- give evidence from the sources that opposes Morag Watt's view.

Your answer **must** be based on all **three** sources.

8

NOW GO TO SECTION 2 ON *PAGE TEN*

MARK

SECTION 2 — SOCIAL ISSUES IN THE UNITED KINGDOM — 20 marks

Attempt ONE part, either

Part C — Social Inequality   on pages 10–13

OR

Part D — Crime and the Law   on pages 14–17

PART C — SOCIAL INEQUALITY

In your answers to Questions 7 and 8 you should give recent examples from the United Kingdom.

Question 7

Groups that experience inequality within society		
Women	Ethnic Minorities	Elderly

Choose **one** of the groups above **or any other group** you have studied.

Describe, **in detail**, **two** ways the Government has tried to reduce the inequalities experienced by the group you have chosen.

4

Question 8

Some people in the UK have a better standard of living than others.

Explain, **in detail**, **two** reasons why some people in the UK have a better standard of living than others.

6

[Turn over for next question]

DO NOT WRITE ON THIS PAGE

PART C (continued)

Question 9

Study Sources 1, 2 and 3 and then answer the question which follows.

You are an adviser to the UK Government. You have been asked to recommend whether the Government should introduce a Fizz Tax on sugary drinks in the UK.

Option 1	Option 2
Introduce a Fizz Tax on sugary drinks	Do not introduce a Fizz Tax on sugary drinks

SOURCE 1

Fizz Tax Factfile

The UK Government is examining a proposal that would see an introduction of an extra 20% Fizz Tax on sugary drinks. These drinks are currently taxed at the standard rate of 20% VAT.

- In the last 10 years the sugar content of drinks has fallen by 9%, but obesity rates have increased by 15%.
- More than 60 organisations back the proposal to introduce a Fizz Tax including the Association for the Study of Obesity and the British Dental Health Association.
- There are over a 100 soft drinks producers in the UK.
- A 20% Fizz Tax per litre would raise £1 billion a year for the NHS.
- 61% of soft drinks now contain no added sugar and the industry is looking at other ways of reducing sugar content and introducing smaller packaging.
- Studies have found that consumption of sugary drinks would only decrease amongst the middle class; the poor within society would not reduce their consumption.
- Tax has been used to discourage smoking and the UK now has one of the lowest smoking rates of 23%.
- Over 14·5 billion litres of soft drinks were consumed in 2013 in the UK.
- A Fizz Tax, according to the British Medical Journal, would reduce the number of obese and overweight people in the UK by 285,000, reduce the number of diabetes cases by 2·4m and see an average adult lose 3·5kg in one year.
- One study found that a 10% tax on sugary drinks could lead to a 7% fall in consumption rate. 20% tax would decrease consumption by 15%.
- In Denmark the Government reversed their Fizz Tax after six months as Danish citizens simply drove across the border into Germany to buy cheaper sugary drinks.

SOURCE 2

Public Opinion Survey on the Introduction of a Fizz Tax in the UK

What is your opinion on the introduction of a "Fizz Tax" on sugary drinks?

5%
20%
28%
24%
23%

☐ Strongly Agree
☐ Agree
■ Disagree
☐ Strongly Disagree
■ No Opinion

How would your consumption of sugary drinks change if the price increased?

17%
30%
18%
35%

☐ Drink Same
☐ Drink Less
☐ Stop Drinking
■ Don't Know

PART C Question 9 (continued)   MARKS

SOURCE 2 (continued)

Obesity Rates in Selected Countries Implementing a Fizz Tax		
Country	Before Fizz Tax Introduced	After Fizz Tax Introduced
Mexico	33%	32%
USA	30%	33%
Denmark	18%	18%
Norway	29%	22%
Hungary	29%	28%
France	19%	18%

SOURCE 3

Viewpoints

There is widespread support for a Fizz Tax on sugary drinks. This is a common strategy used by other countries experiencing an obesity epidemic that has worked. The reality is that the problems associated with the consumption of sugary drinks have created a mini health time bomb in the UK that must be dealt with. Denmark's problems with the Fizz Tax are unlikely to occur in the UK as it is not practical to shop in other countries. The taxing of unhealthy lifestyle choices has clearly worked in the past and the Fizz Tax would undoubtedly lead to a decrease in the consumption of sugary drinks. The money raised from the introduction of this tax could be used to tackle many of the health related issues such as dental decay, diabetes and obesity. It could also be used to provide free and healthy meals to all school children. It would also go a long way to reduce the UK's present obesity rate of 27%.

Ashley Rodgers, Supporter of the Fizz Tax

I strongly believe that the introduction of a Fizz Tax would not help deal with the serious issue of obesity in the UK and is not supported by the general public. Sugary drinks only contribute 2% of the total calories of the average UK diet. One study has found that the introduction of such a tax would have little impact on the groups with the highest rates of obesity, those in deprived communities. The drinks industry recognises it has a role to play in fighting obesity and we have already started to take action. The introduction of a Fizz Tax has not worked in other countries as their obesity rates remain high. The introduction of a Fizz Tax would also discriminate against poorer families who drink more fizzy juice.

Steven Stark, Opponent of the Fizz Tax

You must decide which option to recommend, **either** introduce a Fizz Tax on sugary drinks (**Option 1**) or do not introduce a Fizz Tax on sugary drinks (**Option 2**).

(i) Using Sources 1, 2 and 3, **which option would you choose?**

(ii) Give reasons to **support** your choice.

(iii) **Explain** why you did not choose the other option.

Your answer must be based on all **three** sources.   10

NOW GO TO SECTION 3 ON *PAGE EIGHTEEN*

MARKS

PART D – CRIME AND THE LAW

In your answers to Questions 10 and 11 you should give recent examples from the United Kingdom.

Question 10

Groups that tackle crime in the UK		
Government	Police	Courts

Choose **one** of the groups above or **any other group** you have studied.

Describe, **in detail**, **two** ways in which the group you have chosen has tried to tackle crime in the UK.

4

Question 11

Some people are affected by crime more than others.

Explain, **in detail**, **two** reasons why some people are affected by crime more than others.

6

[Turn over for next question]

DO NOT WRITE ON THIS PAGE

PART D (continued)

Question 12

Study Sources 1, 2 and 3 and then answer the question which follows.

You are a government adviser. You have been asked to recommend **whether** or **not** the United Kingdom Government should ban Legal Highs.

Option 1	Option 2
Ban Legal Highs	Do not ban Legal Highs

SOURCE 1

Legal Highs Factfile

The UK Government is currently examining legislation that will control the sale and use of "legal highs". A legal high contains one or more chemical substances which produce similar effects to illegal drugs, like cocaine, cannabis and ecstasy. These drugs are often included in everyday household products and are often labelled "not for human consumption". Legal highs are often seen as "designer drugs" and can be easily bought and sold online.

- Legal highs are currently not covered by the Misuse of Drugs Act, 1971.
- Some EU countries have already passed legislation controlling the sale and use of legal highs.
- There was a mass demonstration against the proposed legislation due to the inclusion of nitrous oxide, otherwise known as laughing gas, within the bill. Nitrous oxide is commonly used as anaesthetic during dentistry, childbirth and as a mood enhancer.
- Legal highs have been linked to hospital admissions for things such as poisoning, mental health issues, and in extreme cases death.
- Despite the media attention around half of young people have never experimented with legal highs.
- The government are looking at a bill that will make it illegal to sell any "psychoactive substances" other than alcohol, caffeine and nicotine.
- There has been little or no research into the long term or short term risks of taking legal highs.
- The UK has the most severe problem with legal highs in Western Europe, with significant numbers of young people regularly admitting to taking legal highs.
- Many health experts argue banning legal highs will not prevent people taking them; educating people on the danger of these substances would be more beneficial.
- Under the proposed legislation, possession will remain legal so long as there is no intent to supply, the bill could mean up to seven years in prison for people who provide drugs to others.

SOURCE 2

Survey of 16-25 year olds on legal highs

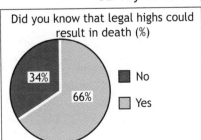

Did you know that legal highs could result in death (%)

34% No
66% Yes

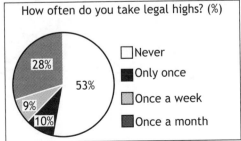

How often do you take legal highs? (%)

28%
53%
9%
10%

Never
Only once
Once a week
Once a month

Page sixteen

MARKS

PART D Question 12 (continued)

SOURCE 2 (continued)

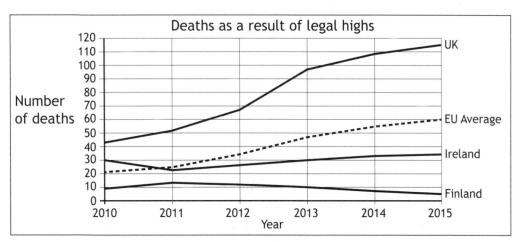

SOURCE 3

Viewpoints

Control and monitoring of legal highs is very difficult. Current laws mean that decisions on whether a product is allowed to be sold are made on a case by case basis. Often new versions are created and sold just as fast as the government can ban them. This makes it difficult to monitor and police.

The government's plan for a blanket ban on legal highs is impractical and not supported by everyone. The Irish government banned legal highs after a number of deaths linked to their use, however this did not reduce deaths and was unsuccessful.

Anna Drummond, Youth Worker

More of my time as a paramedic is being taken up dealing with the consequences of legal highs. The misuse of these drugs diverts our attention from cases that are much more important.

Legal highs are becoming increasingly popular particularly among young people who assume "legal" means "safe". Young people have become much more aware of the health risks of illegal drugs and we see fewer young people addicted to drugs like heroin. However, lots of people are unaware of the dangers of legal highs.

Mandeep Khan, Paramedic

You must decide which option to recommend, **either** ban Legal Highs (**Option 1**) or do not ban Legal Highs (**Option 2**).

(i)   Using Sources 1, 2 and 3, **which option would you choose**?

(ii) Give reasons to **support** your choice.

(iii) **Explain** why you did not choose the other option.

Your answer must be based on all **three** sources.

10

NOW GO TO SECTION 3 ON *PAGE EIGHTEEN*

MARKS

SECTION 3 — INTERNATIONAL ISSUES — 20 marks

Attempt ONE part, either

Part E — World Powers   on pages 18–21

OR

Part F — World Issues   on pages 22–25

PART E — WORLD POWERS

In your answers to Questions 13 and 14 you should give recent examples from a world power you have studied.

Question 13

> The citizens of every world power have political rights.

Describe, **in detail**, **two** political rights that the citizens have in the world power you have studied.

In your answer you **must** state the world power you have studied.   6

Question 14

> World powers have the ability to influence other countries.

Explain, **in detail**, **two** reasons why the world power you have studied has the ability to influence other countries.

In your answer you **must** state the world power you have studied.   6

[Turn over for next question]

DO NOT WRITE ON THIS PAGE

PART E (continued)

Question 15

Study Sources 1, 2 and 3 and then answer the question which follows.

SOURCE 1

Problems facing Japan in 2015

Many people think Japan is in crisis. Its problems include a weak economy, radiation from nuclear power plants, an extremely unpopular government and a rapidly changing population structure. All of these things are long term problems which are affecting Japanese standards of living.

Since the economic crisis that hit the world in 2008, low incomes have become a problem. It is estimated that 16% of all Japanese people are living below the poverty line. Many large electronics companies have seen their profits fall. Average income went from 37,185 US dollars in 2008 to 34,822 US dollars in 2011.

One third of single women now live in poverty. Although 12 million women work, over half are in part-time jobs, receiving small salaries. Increased poverty and a different population structure will make old age pensions and elderly care very expensive in the future. By the middle of this century over one third of the population will be collecting their old age pension.

Despite all the problems facing modern Japan, many people point to its strengths. It had 22 crimes per 1,000 people in 2014. It remains the third largest economy in the world where some people still enjoy an extremely high standard of living.

SOURCE 2

	People in poverty (%)	Crimes per 1000 people	Home ownership (%)	Internet access per 1000 people
Germany	15	79	44	841
Argentina	30	36	67	599
South Korea	16·5	32	54	865
Italy	19·6	39	74	585
France	8	61	64	819
European Union	8	80	71	848

Additional statistics – Selected Countries

PART E Question 15 (continued)

SOURCE 2 (continued)

MARKS

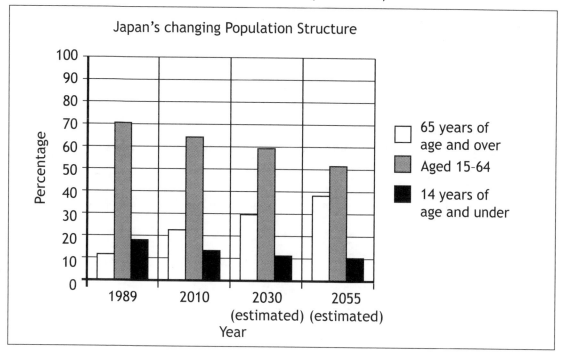

Japan's changing Population Structure

Legend:
- 65 years of age and over
- Aged 15-64
- 14 years of age and under

SOURCE 3

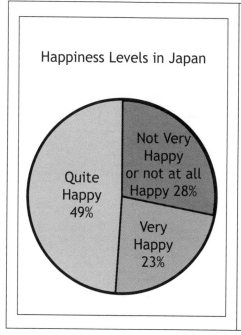

Happiness Levels in Japan

- Quite Happy 49%
- Not Very Happy or not at all Happy 28%
- Very Happy 23%

Better Life Index Study

According to the Better Life Index, the citizens of the world's third largest economy are not very happy even though Japan is one of the safest places in the world to live.

Japan boasts one of the highest life expectancies in the world at 83 years. In future this may be difficult to maintain as the proportion of the population paying tax falls.

The country continues to be at the forefront of the electronics industry which employs many people. Of every 1000 Japanese people, 865 have access to the internet. Just over three quarters of Japanese people say they are satisfied with their home. 61% of Japanese people own their own homes but housing has become much more expensive for young people due to the growing numbers of older people.

Using Sources 1, 2 and 3, what **conclusions** can be drawn.

You should reach a conclusion about each of the following:

- The problem of crime in Japan compared to other countries.
- The effects of the changing population structure in Japan.
- The country most like Japan.

Your conclusions must be supported by evidence from the sources. You should link information within and between the sources in support of your conclusions.

Your answer must be based on all **three** sources.

8

MARK

PART F — WORLD ISSUES

In your answers to Questions 16 and 17 you should give recent examples from a world issue you have studied.

Question 16

> People are affected by international conflicts and issues in many different ways.

Describe, **in detail**, **two** ways in which people have been affected by an international conflict or issue you have studied.

6

Question 17

> The attempts of international organisations to tackle conflicts and issues are sometimes unsuccessful.

Explain, **in detail**, **two** reasons why international organisations have **either** been successful **or** unsuccessful in tackling an international conflict or issue you have studied.

6

[Turn over for next question]

DO NOT WRITE ON THIS PAGE

PART F (continued)

Question 18

Study Sources 1, 2 and 3 and then answer the question which follows.

SOURCE 1

Ambiona outbreak in Central America 2014 : Factfile

Ambiona virus is a severe and often fatal illness in humans. The virus is transmitted to people from monkeys and spreads in the human population through human-to-human transmission.

The outbreak in Central America in 2014 involved major urban and rural areas of three different countries. At the moment 7% of Country X have contracted the virus, 16% of Country Y's population has the virus and 2% of Country Z have the virus.

Current life expectancy in Country X is 55 years, Country Y is 59 and in Country Z it is 62.

In 2014, world governments set three aid targets to fight the Ambiona outbreak in Central America:

- The first aid target was to raise almost $1,000 million in financial aid to combat the Ambiona crisis by 2017.
- The second aid target was to employ a further 100 trained nurses in each of the three countries.
- The third aid target was to limit the number of deaths caused by Ambiona to 4,000.

The additional aid they require is to be used to carefully check for any new cases, undertake further medical research into the Ambiona virus, ensure safe burials and further educate the population about the illness. It would also be used to provide quality care from qualified medical staff which can improve a patient's chance of survival and protective clothing for medical staff to prevent the spread of the disease.

SOURCE 2

Health and Social Statistics in Central American Countries (December 2014)

Country	Number of Ambiona Cases	Number of Deaths from Ambiona	Death Rates from Ambiona (%)	Literacy Rate (%)
Country X	2,283	1,412	62	72
Country Y	7,719	3,177	41	77
Country Z	7,650	1,742	23	83

PART F Question 18 (continued)   MARKS

SOURCE 3

World News

By the end of 2014, several Central American countries reported numerous cases of Ambiona which had led to a significant number of deaths. The health care services in these countries have been placed under great strain as they struggle to control the outbreak of the virus. World leaders have responded in setting aid targets and donating resources to help deal with the crisis.

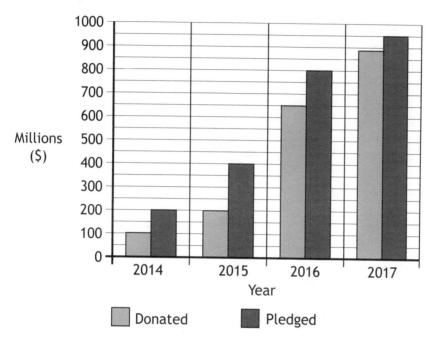

Up to 2013, Country Z attracted a high number of foreign visitors leading to a successful tourist industry where many people were employed. The average income in 2013 was $9876 compared to near neighbours Country X (6767) and Country Y (5654). However, the devastating Ambiona outbreak in 2014 has led to a slump in the tourist industry. Hotels have closed, the number of foreign visitors has sharply fallen and many workers have lost their jobs.

Using Sources 1, 2 and 3, what **conclusions** can be drawn.

You should reach a conclusion about each of the following:

- The progress in achieving the world governments' first aid target.
- The Central American country most affected by the Ambiona outbreak in 2014.
- The relationship between the standard of living and Ambiona death rates.

Your conclusions must be supported by evidence from the sources. You should link information within and between the sources in support of your conclusions.

Your answer must be based on all **three** sources.   8

[END OF QUESTION PAPER]

[BLANK PAGE]

DO NOT WRITE ON THIS PAGE

NATIONAL 5

Answers

NATIONAL 5 MODERN STUDIES 2014

Section 1

Part A: Democracy in Scotland

1. *Candidates can be credited in a number of ways up to a maximum of 6 marks.*

Possible approaches to answering the question:

The Scottish Parliament has control over devolved powers in Scotland like health, education and housing.
[2 marks for a list answer which lacks any detail]

The Scottish Parliament has a range of devolved powers. One of the main ones is education. Scottish pupils sit Nationals and Highers whereas English students sit GCSEs.
[2 marks single point with an example]

Holyrood has control over many devolved areas such as health care. The Scottish government has been able to create different laws in Scotland eg the Smoking Ban in 2006 and the plan to have a minimum price for alcohol.
[3 marks developed point with exemplification]

Reference to aspects of the following will be credited:
• The power to make law
• Agriculture, forestry and fishing
• Education & training
• Health & social services
• Housing
• Law & order

2. *Candidates can be credited in a number of ways up to a maximum of 6 marks.*

Possible approaches to answering the question:

People may feel it is their right to vote and that they should therefore use it.
[1 mark for a limited answer which lacks any detail.]

Many people are members of political parties such as the Scottish National Party and so vote for their candidate.
[2 marks for a single point with an example]

Many people in Scotland feel that it is not only a right but also a responsibility that they should vote to uphold democracy. If many thousands of Scots decide not to vote then the result of an election may not be representative. In 2011 almost 40% didn't vote, if they had, the SNP may not have won.
[3 marks for a developed point with exemplification]

Reference to aspects of the following will be credited:
• Basic right in a democracy
• Right denied to citizens elsewhere in the world
• Desire to see own party succeed
• Wish to ensure another party is not elected.
• Right denied to women until early last century
• Feel electoral system reflects their views

3. *Candidates can be credited in a number of ways up to a maximum of 8 marks.*

Possible approaches to answering the question:

The importance of Trade Union donations to party election campaigns.

Conclusion – Trade Union contributions were not very important to political parties during the election in 2011. [1 mark for valid conclusion]
Evidence – Trade Unions contributed 29% of the overall donations to political parties in 2011 compared to 41% from individuals [Source 3]
The SNP and Conservatives rely more on wealthy business people and as such unions are not important to them [Source 1]

Conclusion – They are much more important to Labour than the other parties [1 mark for valid conclusion]

Evidence – 29% is almost a third of all party donations – Labour however is more reliant as over a third of their funding is from trade unions (36%). [Sources 1 and 3]

The link between a party's election spending and election success.

Conclusion – The party which spends the most wins the election. [1 mark for a valid conclusion]

Evidence – In 2007, SNP spent the most at c£3.5 million compared to Labour at £1.6 million [Source 2] and they won the election by 1 seat [Source 3]
In 2011, SNP spent the most at c£2.6 million compared to Labour's £1.1 million [Source 2] and the SNP won 69 seats compared to 37 for Labour [Source 3].

The link between election spending and voter awareness of election campaign methods.

Conclusion – There is a direct link between election spending and voter awareness of campaign methods. [1 mark for valid conclusion]

Evidence – Spending on leaflets increased from £1.2 million to £1.4 million between 2007 and 2011 and awareness of leaflets increased from 89% to 93% of voters. [Source 1]

Conclusion – Money spent on campaign methods means people are more aware of it. [1 mark for valid conclusion]

Evidence – In 2011, the smallest sum (only £47,000) was spent on rallies and public meetings and only 2% of people attended these (this is the smallest number). [Source 1]

Part B: Democracy in the United Kingdom

1. *Candidates can be credited in a number of ways up to a maximum of 6 marks.*

Possible approaches to answering the question:

The UK Parliament has reserved powers in Scotland like defence and immigration.
[1 mark for a list answer which lacks any detail]

One of the main reserved powers is the benefit system eg child benefit is the same in Edinburgh and London.
[2 marks for a single point with an example]

The UK Parliament has a range of reserved powers which affect Scotland. One of these is defence. The UK government has power over the size and location of Scottish forces eg in 2013 Leuchars air base was reduced in size and changed to an army base.
[3 marks for a developed point with exemplification]

Reference to aspects of the following will be credited:
• The power to make law
• Immigration

- Benefits & social security
- Defence
- Foreign policy
- Nuclear power

2. *Candidates can be credited in a number of ways* **up to a maximum of 6 marks.**

Possible approaches to answering the question:

People may feel it is their right to vote and that they should therefore use it.

> [1 mark for a limited answer which lacks any detail.]

Many people are members of political parties such as the Labour Party and so vote for their candidate.

> [2 marks for a single point with an example]

Many people in the UK feel that it is not only a right but also a responsibility that they should vote to uphold democracy. If many thousands of Scots decide not to vote then the result of an election may not be representative. Eg In 2010 approx one third of people didn't vote in the general election. If they had, the coalition may not have been necessary.

> [3 marks for a developed point with exemplification]

Reference to aspects of the following will be credited:
- Basic right in a democracy
- People likely to participate in a General Election
- Right denied to citizens elsewhere in the world
- Desire to see own party succeed
- Wish to ensure another party is not elected
- Right denied to women until early last century

3. *Candidates can be credited in a number of ways* **up to a maximum of 8 marks.**

Possible approaches to answering the question:

The importance of trade union donations to party election campaigns.

Conclusion – trade union contributions were not very important to political parties during the election in 2010.

> [1 mark for valid conclusion]

Evidence –
Trade unions contributed 16% of the overall donations to political parties in 2010 compared to 47% from individuals [Source 3]
The Labour Party received 36% of their funding from Unions but this is less than half so not that important [Source 1]
The Conservatives rely on wealthy business people so Unions are not important to them [Source 1]

Conclusion – trade unions are more important to Labour than the other parties. [1 mark valid conclusion]

Evidence –
16% of all party donations [Source 3]
Labour however is more reliant as over a third of their funding is from trade unions (36%) [Source 1]

The link between a party's election spending and election success.

Conclusion – The party which spends the most wins the election. [1 mark valid conclusion]

Evidence –
In 2005 Labour spent the most at c£18 million compared to Conservatives at £17 million [Source 2] and they won the election by 158 seats [Source 3]
In 2010 Conservatives spent the most at c£16 million compared to Labour's £8 million [Source 2] and the Conservatives won 307 seats compared to 258 for Labour [Source 3].

The link between election spending and voter awareness of election campaign methods.

Conclusion – As election spending on campaign methods decreases so does voter awareness of these methods [1 mark valid conclusion]

Evidence – In 2005, £15 million was spent on billboard advertising and this fell to £9 million in 2010 [Source 1] Awareness of billboard advertising fell from 62% in 2005 to 48% in 2010. [Source 1]

Conclusion – More money spent on a campaign method means people are more aware of it, eg leaflets [1 mark valid conclusion]

Evidence – In 2010, most money (£12.3 million) was spent on leaflets and 93% of people had received leaflets. [Source 1]
Only 1.7 million was spent on public meetings and only 2% of people attended one in 2010 [Source 1]

Section 2

Part C: Social Inequality

1. *Candidates can be credited in a number of ways* **up to a maximum of 4 marks.**

Possible approaches to answering the question:

The Government has tried to tackle inequality by providing benefits.

> [1 mark – accurate but undeveloped point]

The Government has tried to tackle inequality by providing more apprenticeships.

> [1 mark – accurate but undeveloped point]

The Voluntary sector has tried to tackle inequality by providing financial support to vulnerable groups such as children. Cash for Kids is a children's charity that raises money for disadvantaged children.

> [2 marks – accurate with development]

The Government has introduced the Universal Credit to tackle inequality. This benefit was introduced in October 2013. Universal Credit is a single payment that merges a number of benefits together to make them easier to claim. For example, Universal Credit helps to pay childcare costs and allow parents to work.

> [3 marks – accurate point with development and exemplification]

GOVERNMENT
- **All major benefits provided by Central Government including:** Universal Credit; Attendance Allowance; Disability Living Allowance, Carers Allowance etc
- **Elderly Benefits:** Pension Credits; Winter Fuel payment; Cold Weather Payments and free TV Licence for over 75yrs
- **Council Tax Benefit:** Helps to meet the financial needs of low income groups by providing a reduction in their Council Tax bill
- **Families:** Free School Meals; School Clothing vouchers, Maternity Allowance and Educational Maintenance Allowance (EMA)
- **Disability Living Allowance** (Known from April 2013 as Person Independence Payments): Paid to those under 65 who have extra costs created by a disability
- **Recent legislation** e.g. Childcare Act [2006], Equality Act [2010]

INDIVIDUALS

- Taking individual responsibility for circumstances
- Working hard at school, college & university
- Undertaking voluntary work to gain skills/experience
- Contributing to charity – altruistic actions
- Setting a good example for peers/friends/family
- Making full use of government help eg training schemes or Job Centre Plus

VOLUNTARY SECTOR

- **Charities:** groups such as Barnardo's, Enable Scotland, Glasgow's Children's Holiday Scheme or Glasgow the Caring City who help the most vulnerable in society
- **Housing Associations:** Non-profit making organisations that provide low cost social housing
- **Credit Unions:** Providing low cost loans and mortgages to its members

PRIVATE SECTOR

- **Retail/Shops:** Providing special discount days for vulnerable groups eg B&Q Pensioners' discount
- **Leisure Facilities:** Concession and reduced gym membership rates for students, pensioners and families. Special family meals deal in restaurants
- **Private Schools/Nurseries:** Reduced fees for more than one child
- **Supermarkets:** Introduction of low cost/value brand fruit and vegetables

2. *Candidates can be credited in a number of ways **up to a maximum of 8 marks**.*

Possible approaches to answering the question:

Some people live in poverty because they don't have a job.

> [1 mark – accurate but undeveloped point]

Some people live in poverty because they have lost their job because of a recession.

> [2 marks – accurate point with development]

Some people live in poverty because they lack qualifications. This might be because they did not try hard at school and did not pass any exams. This makes it harder for them to find a job that is well paid, so might only be able to get work in lower paid jobs such as working in a shop.

> [3 marks – accurate point with development and exemplification]

Some people live in poverty because of their family type. For example, a lone parent family may be more at risk from poverty than a family that has two working parents. Also many lone parent families are headed by women who tend to get paid less than men. Lone parents might live in poverty because they are dependent on benefits as it might be difficult for them to find work with hours suitable or pay for childcare when working.

> [4 marks – relevant, accurate point with development, analysis and exemplification]

Reference to aspects of the following will be credited:

- **Occupations:** Some people have well-paid jobs such as professionals, while others may work in lower paid occupations
- **Recession:** Some people might lose their jobs during a recession. The jobs that are normally affected first are lower paid service sector jobs
- **Long-term unemployment:** Some groups such as NEETs may never have had a job, and subsequently find it difficult to get a job without experience so remain on benefits and unemployed

- **Educational attainment:** Some people leave school with no or few qualifications, which means they cannot enter further or higher education. This means that they don't have the same earning potential as someone who has gone to college or university so will generally be paid less
- **Household Structure:** A household with one adult is more likely to live in poverty than a household with two adults
- **Lack of skills:** Some people, for example the elderly, may not have skills appropriate to the job market, eg IT skills, so find it difficult to find employment
- **Ill health:** Some people may have long-term health problems that mean they cannot work or have to give up work because of poor health, eg cancer sufferers
- **Social problems:** Some people experience social problems such as addictions to drugs and alcohol that may affect their ability to find or hold down a stable job. Other social problems such as involvement in crime may push a person into poverty if they have a criminal record they might find it harder to get a job
- **Race:** Ethnic minorities still experience prejudice and discrimination. Those with language difficulties might find it difficult to get a job, and therefore have difficulty accessing a decent level of income. Poverty rates amongst ethnic minorities are higher than whites
- **Gender:** More women work part-time or in lower paid jobs. Also wage inequality means women are paid on average 15% less than men, so lowering their earning potential
- **Age and disability:** The elderly have higher poverty rates as many rely solely on the state retirement pension. Disability poverty levels are also higher than average poverty rates as 30% of disabled adults live in poverty compared to 20% of the overall adult population

3. *Candidates can be credited in a number of ways **up to a maximum of 8 marks**.*

Possible approaches to answering the question:

Sophie Wilson is supported (not selective) in her view **"There have been great improvements in the UK's health in the last 10 years."**

Candidates should give evidence from the Sources that supports Sophie Wilson's view.

Sophie's view is supported (not selective) by Source 1 which shows that life expectancy has increased.

> [1 mark – accurate use of Source 1 but minimal development]

Sophie's view is supported (not selective) by Source 1 which shows that life expectancy has increased in the last 10 years from 77 years to 80 years because we are making better lifestyle choices.

> [2 marks – accurate use of Source 1 and detailed use of statistics]

Sophie's view is supported (not selective) by Source 1 which shows people are making better lifestyles choices. This is supported by Source 2 that shows the number of people smoking has decreased by 5% for both men and women in the last 10 years. This has also led to a decrease in the number of heart attacks associated with smoking. This shows that the UK's health has improved.

> [3 marks – accurate information from two Sources with some evaluation of the statistics, ie '..this shows the UK's health has improved.']

Reference to aspects of the following will be credited:
- People are eating more healthily and exercising more (Source 1)
- Big decrease in death rates compared to other countries (Source 1)
- Smoking rates for men and women have fallen (Source 2) because Government outlawed smoking in public places (Source 3)
- The number of admissions to hospitals has decreased, these include children's asthmas admissions from 26,969 cases in 2006 to 20,167 cases in 2013 (Source 3)
- The Government has worked hard to improve the health of the nation (Source 1) by passing laws banning smoking in public places (Source 3)

Sophie Wilson is opposed (selective) in her view **"There have been great improvements in the UK's health in the last 10 years."**

Candidates should give evidence from the Sources that oppose Sophie Wilson's view.

Sophie's view is opposed (selective) as Source 1 shows many doctors warn that more has to be done to tackle the growing problem of childhood obesity and the health problems it causes. This is supported by Source 2 that shows the number of adults who are classed as obese has also risen over the last 10 years, with a 5% increase in Scotland and a 4% increase in England. This shows that health relating to obesity has not improved over the last 10 years.

[3 marks – accurate information from two Sources with some evaluation of the statistics, ie '..this shows Britain's health has not improved..']

Reference to aspects of the following will be credited:
- Source 1 shows that obesity is a big problem in the UK
- Britain's health still poor compared with other Western European Countries (Source 1)
- Since 2004, the number of obese children suffering from diabetes has doubled (Source 1)
- Obesity rates in Scotland and in England are increasing (Source 2)
- Approximately one in five adults continue to smoke in the UK (Source 3), with male smoking rates constantly higher than female rates (Source 2)
- Source 3 shows that people are still making bad health choices, especially in Scotland with 27% of adults smoking and up to 40% in deprived inner city areas. (Source 3)

Part D: Crime and the Law

1. *Candidates can be credited in a number of ways* **up to a maximum of 4 marks.**

Possible approaches to answering the question:

The Children's Hearing System can help young people by taking them away from their home. (1 mark)

The Children's Hearing System tries to deal with the reasons why young people commit crime and offers support for them to stop offending. (2 marks)

The Children's Hearing System helps young people by providing a relaxed atmosphere where young people can discuss their offending behaviour. It is less intimidating than going to an adult court and they will get help and support from school, social workers and the police to change their behaviour. (3 marks)

Reference to aspects of the following will be credited:
- Targets both offending behaviour and welfare concerns
- Impartial, voluntary panel makes decisions
- Safe environment to discuss issues and problems
- Tries to deal with root cause of problems
- Input from various agencies eg police, social work, schools
- Power to remove "at risk" children from their homes
- Can refer to secure accommodation or court if necessary

2. *Candidates can be credited in a number of ways* **up to a maximum of 8 marks.**

Possible approaches to answering the question:

Prisons don't reduce reoffending because you learn how to commit more crimes when you are inside. (1 mark)

Electronic tags are a good way of reducing reoffending as if you have a job you can still go but are punished with a curfew at night (2 marks)

Many prisons don't have enough staff or money to run effective rehabilitation programmes which means that some offenders are released with the same addictions they had when they went in to prison. (3 marks)

Community Service Orders have been very successful in reducing reoffending as they make the offender pay something back to the community. This could involve painting a children's playground which makes the offender feel they have done something good that others will benefit from. This can change the negative feelings many offenders have and give them back some pride and self-esteem which will make them less likely to commit another crime. (4 marks)

Reference to aspects of the following will be credited:
- High levels of re-offending lead to belief that prison doesn't work
- Prisons are expensive and overcrowded
- Few opportunities for rehabilitation in prisons
- Success of Drug Courts and Drug Treatment and Testing Orders (DTTOs)
- Electronic tagging allows offenders to stay at home, continue working and maintain family relationships
- Success of Community Service Orders (CSOs)
- High levels of success for Restorative Justice especially among young people and first-time offenders
- Too many short sentences which fail to rehabilitate as well as a community sentence would

3. *Candidates can be credited in a number of ways* **up to a maximum of 8 marks.**

Possible approaches to answering the question:

Oliver Thomson is supported (not selective) in his view, **"Victims of crime in Scotland receive satisfactory support."**

Candidates should give evidence from the Sources that support Oliver Thomson's view.

Oliver Thomson's view is supported (not selective) because it says Surveys show that victims are satisfied with the help and support given to them as victims of crime. This is supported by Source two which says that 69% of victims are happy with police support and further that 74% were happy with Victim Support Scotland. Both of these figures show a significant majority of victims who are satisfied. (3 marks – accurate information from two parts of Source 2 with some evaluative terminology used regarding the statistic included, ie "significant majority")

Reference to aspects of the following will be credited:
- Victim Support Scotland (VSS) is a voluntary group which provides a listening service for victims. Their volunteers can be easily contacted by phone, email or face to face (Source 1)
- The Victims and Witnesses Bill, proposes a "victim surcharge", meaning that those who commit crimes will contribute to the cost of providing support to victims eg house alarm systems and travel costs to hospital (Source 1 and 3)
- Over £5 million per year is provided by the Scottish Government to support Victim Support Scotland and they have committed to maintaining that level of funding (Source 1)
- The Scottish Government has made a very positive attempt to support victims of crime in introducing the Victim and Witness Bill (Source 3)
- Victims on the whole are happy with the support they get from voluntary groups and the police (Source 3)

Oliver Thomson is opposed (selective) in his view, "Victims of crime in Scotland receive satisfactory support."

Candidates should give evidence from the Sources that oppose Oliver Thomson's view.

Oliver's view is opposed (selective) as the Scottish Victim Crisis Centre is a voluntary group which has a 9 month waiting list for victims who wish to talk about their experiences of crime (1 mark – accurate use of Source 1 but no development).

Oliver's view is opposed (selective) as the Scottish Victim Crisis Centre is a voluntary group which has a 9 month waiting list for victims who wish to talk about their experiences of crime. This is supported by Source 3 which says the funding given to some voluntary groups is simply not enough to support the level of demand for services such as counselling and advice. (2 marks – evidence linked from Sources 1 and 3).

Reference to aspects of the following will be credited:
- Victim Support volunteers are not trained counsellors and can only give practical information (Source 1)
- Funding is so low in the Scottish Victim Crisis Centre that victims often get an engaged tone or an answering machine (Source 1)
- The Scottish Government give the Scottish Victim Crisis Centre £50,000 a year but staff say this is nowhere near enough to meet the demand for their services (Source 1)
- The funding given to some voluntary groups is simply not enough to support the level of demand for services such as counselling and advice (Source 3)
- Some voluntary groups are not able to give full training to their staff as they can't afford it (Source 3)

Section 3

Part E: World Powers

1. *Candidates can be credited in a number of ways up to a maximum of 4 marks.*

Possible approaches to answering the question:

USA
- In America, Barack Obama introduced a new health-care law
  [1 mark – accurate point]
- In America, Barack Obama introduced a new health-care law to try and help poor people get health care
  [2 marks – developed point]

- In America, Barack Obama introduced a new health-care law called the Affordable Care Act. Lots of Americans cannot afford private health care, especially people on low incomes who tend to be ethnic minorities. The act forces people to get health care or they will be fined
  [3 marks – accurate point with development and exemplification]

Reference to aspects of the following will be credited:
- Medicare, Medicaid and State Children's Health Insurance Program (covers children who do not qualify for Medicaid)
- Temporary Assistance for Needy Families (TANF)
- Affirmative Action programmes as they apply today eg the Supreme Court has basically ruled that consideration of an applicant's race/ethnicity is legal
- American Recovery and Reinvestment Act 2009 – provides expansion of unemployment benefits, social welfare provision, education and health care
- No Child Left Behind (NCLB) 2001 – aimed to improve performance in public schools to improve qualifications/employability of all children. Backed with big increases in federal funding but on-going debate as to success
- Race to the Top is a $4.35 billion United States Department of Education contest created to spur innovation and reforms in state and local district education. It is funded as part of the American Recovery and Reinvestment Act of 2009
- Food stamps now known as Supplemental Nutrition Assistance Programme (SNAP) to provide healthy food for poor families
- Federal minimum wage

CHINA
- Today most farms operate as private businesses and decisions about what to produce and how to produce are made by farmers. The government created the Household Responsibility System. Farmers have to give a certain amount to the government, but any surplus is kept by the farmer. This means that poor farmers are allowed to sell their goods for a profit thus reducing inequality
  [3 marks – accurate point with development and exemplification]

Reference to aspects of the following will be credited:
- Dismantling of work permit system (hukou)
- Foreign investment, encouragement of private business (Open Door Policy and Special Economic Zones)
- Encouraging rural areas and small towns to develop entrepreneurs and industrial growth (Township and Village Enterprises)
- Development of social security system
- Better rights for women
- Improving health services, housing and reducing crime

SOUTH AFRICA
Reference to aspects of the following will be credited:
- Affirmative Action
- Black Economic Empowerment (BEE)
- Programmes to ensure everyone has access to drinkable water, sanitation and electricity
- Land redistribution policy

2. *Candidates can be credited in a number of ways up to a maximum of 6 marks.*

Possible approaches to answering the question:

USA
Participation of Hispanics is unequal due to language barriers.
  [1 mark – accurate point]

Participation of African Americans/Hispanics is unequal because levels of representation are poor especially at Federal Government level. This leads to a lack of positive ethnic minority role models. Some limited progress has been made, eg election of Barack Obama but there have been 43 white Presidents and only 1 black president. Many African/Hispanic Americans simply view politics as a "a white man's game".

[4 marks – relevant, accurate point with development, analysis and exemplification]

- Many ethnic minorities feel their vote doesn't matter as they have not seen much improvement in their living conditions/economic position
- Relationship between participation and poorer levels of education
- Growing up in poor conditions, leads to lower levels of engagement with politics so they are less likely to vote, stand as candidates, join political parties
- Hispanics: English might not be their main language but the language of politics is English. Cannot access political debate, campaigns, etc
- The process of registering to vote can be time-consuming, and varies from state to state. It is easy to be confused or put off by the registration forms

Participation of women:
- Traditional view of women as mother, home maker means women don't see politics as a career. Do not have the same level of political ambition/ feel they have to choose one or the other. These views are prevalent amongst religious groups.
- More likely to be lone parents so have other issues to concern them.
- Lack of positive role models.
- Media coverage of female politicians puts some women off, eg Sarah Palin's and Hillary Clinton's treatment by the press was viewed as sexist with too much focus on appearance.

CHINA
- Membership of the Communist Party is strictly controlled and is not an option for many groups (One – Party system)
- Citizens can only vote at local level. Only candidates and parties sanctioned by the Communist Party are allowed to seek election. Eight other parties are legal but do not act as "opposition" eg China Democratic League, Chinese Peasants' and Workers' Democratic Party
- Organisations that have opposed the Communist Party have been banned as dangerous and subversive, eg China Democracy Party, National Democratic Party of Tibet
- Organisations like the Falun Gong and the independence movements for Taiwan and Tibet have also been banned and their members persecuted
- Some pressure group activity is allowed but it cannot question the authority or legitimacy of the Communist Party. Many dissidents have been in prison since Tiananmen Square and others have been exiled eg Wei Jingsheng
- Independent trade unions are not permitted. The Federation of Trade Unions is linked to the Communist Party. There has been some limited progress eg improved pay and conditions for Apple workers
- Environmental groups have grown in number eg many campaigned against the building of the Three Gorges Dam. These groups have experienced limited success and have become popular

- Discrimination stops many women taking part in politics. Attitudes have been slow to change and few women stand as candidates. The All-China Women's Federation (linked to Communist Party) campaigns to promote equality

3. *Candidates can be credited in a number of ways **up to a maximum of 10 marks**.*

Possible approaches to answering the question:

OPTION 1

Australia should keep compulsory voting as more people vote.

[1 mark – evidence from Source 1]

Source 1 points out that compulsory voting is widely supported among Australian people and the pie chart shows 65% do not want to get rid of it.

[2 marks – evidence linked from Source 1 and Source 3]

Turnout is higher in Australia with compulsory voting – it was only 47% before it was introduced and now it is around 95% – supported by evidence in Source 2 where turnout at the most recent parliamentary election was 93.22%. Turnout has doubled since it was introduced.

[3 marks – evaluative terminology, evidence linked from Source 1 and 2]

Reference to aspects of the following will be credited:
- The Australian Prime Minister wants to keep compulsory voting (Source 3).
- Result is more accurate when everyone has participated (Source 3).

Reasons for rejecting the other option:

In all countries where there is compulsory voting, turnout is much higher compared to all countries where there isn't eg Brazil and Argentina have turnout rates near 80% while Canada and Russia have only 60%.

[3 marks – detailed evidence with evaluative comments from Source 2]

OPTION 2

Australia should get rid of compulsory voting as it is undemocratic to force people to vote.

[1 mark – evidence from Source 1]

People with little interest in politics are forced to the polls (Source 1) and (Source 3). "People who aren't interested should not be required to vote – bad decisions in the voting booth contribute to bad government."

[2 marks – evidence linked from Source 1 and 3]

Resources must be allocated to determine whether those who failed to vote have "valid and sufficient" reasons. Source 1 also says "millions of dollars are spent on checking up on those who didn't turn up." In the state of Queensland almost $1 million in state funds has been allocated to chase up those who failed to vote. This is a lot of money.

[3 marks – evidence linked from Source 1 and 3]

Reference to aspects of the following will be credited:
- It's unfair to punish people for not voting – only 37% of people think you should be fined (Source 1)
- Some people cannot get to polling stations due to genuine reasons ("poor people don't have a way to get to their voting place unlike rich people who have cars.") (Source 3)

Reasons for rejecting the other option:
Eileen Smith in Source 3 says "Forcing the population to vote means they will just deliberately spoil their ballot papers to avoid a fine" and in Source 2 it is clear that in

all of the countries with compulsory voting, the number of informal ballot papers are much higher (eg in Brazil it is 8.64% compared to only 0.7% in Canada). Source 1 shows that 9% of Australians have at some point registered an informal vote.
[3 marks – evaluative terminology, detailed evidence from Sources 1, 2 and 3]

Part F: World Issues

1. *Candidates can be credited in a number of ways* **up to a maximum of 4 marks.**

   Possible approaches to answering the question:

   Organisations send aid to help starving people. (1 mark)

   The UN provide tents and medicines for refugees. (2 marks)

   Charities such as the Red Cross provide experts such as doctors and nurses to areas where natural disasters have occurred, eg they spent many millions of pounds on field hospitals to help the victims of the typhoon in the Philippines. (3 marks)

   Reference to aspects of the following will be credited: (Answers may vary greatly depending on the international conflict or issue studied.)
   • Food/water/emergency relief
   • Medical equipment/experts/medicines/vaccinations
   • Peace talks/treaty negotiations
   • Economic sanctions
   • UN resolutions
   • Economic Aid
   • Specialist workers – engineers, scientists etc
   • Financial Aid through the world bank
   • UN may hold peace talks, eg with Syrian government during times of conflict. Pressure for government to resign

2. *Candidates can be credited in a number of ways* **up to a maximum of 6 marks.**

   Possible approaches to answering the question:

   HIV/Aids is caused by poor education. (1 mark)

   Terrorism usually happens when a group of people feel they have been badly treated by a government. For example the Boston bombings were carried out by people who thought they had been unfairly treated by the USA. (2 marks)

   Piracy is a major problem especially off the north east coast of Africa. Many poor people in Somalia are forced or persuaded to hi-jack ships and to take hostages by local gangs. There can be more money in it than there is in fishing. (3 marks)

   Reference to aspects of the following will be credited:
   • War in Afghanistan – response to terror/establish democracy
   • The "Arab Spring" – demand for human rights, impact of internet
   • International Debt – corruption, poverty, war, Western banks
   • Poverty/Famine – natural disaster, war, climate, corruption, unfair trade
   • Illegal immigration – poverty, famine, war

3. *Candidates can be credited in a number of ways* **up to a maximum of 10 marks.**

   Possible approaches to answering the question:

OPTION 1

NATO should send troops to Country A as 140 000 people have been killed.
[1 mark – evidence from Source 1]

Source 1 points out that free elections were never held and that many people see democracy as the solution. Andy N from source three agrees that democracy is the solution.
[2 marks – evidence linked from Source 1 and Source 3]

It is believed that the President has used chemical weapons to kill 600 of his own people (S1). David W argues that we cannot stand by and watch this happen and a massive majority of 85% of those asked in Source 2 agree that NATO should do everything it can to stop chemical weapons.
[3 mark – evaluative terminology, evidence linked from Source 1, 2 and 3]

Reference to aspects of the following will be credited:
• The people want democratic reform (Sources 1 and/or 3)
• Many civilians have been killed (Sources 1 and/or 3).
• It worked in Libya, so why not in Country A? ie NATO got rid of Gaddafi (Source 3)
• People want chemical attacks stopped (Sources 2 and 3)
• NATO needs friendly Middle Eastern governments (Sources 1 and/or 2)

Reasons for rejecting the other option:
Source one tells us that the UK and the USA would like a friendlier government in Country A. 59% (a majority) of those asked in Source 2 agree that this is vital for NATO, so option 2 (doing nothing) is not a good option.
(3 marks – evidence from two sources with an evaluative comment.)

OPTION 2

NATO should not send troops to Country A as 54% of the public strongly disagree.
[1 mark – evidence from Source 2]

NATO should not send troops to Country A as the majority of those questioned think that NATO cannot afford it. 27% agree and 42% strongly agree, this is well over half.
[2 marks – evidence from Source 2 with evaluative comment]

The vast majority, 83% think that sending NATO troops to Country A would not help the refugees (Source 2). Two million refugees really need help as they are living in terrible conditions (Source 3). So option two should not be followed.
[3 marks – evidence linked from Source 2 and 3 with evaluative comment]

Reference to aspects of the following will be credited:
• Cost is too high (Source 2 and Source 3)
• More troops make things worse (Source 1, Source 2 and Source 3)
• Wouldn't help refugees (Source 2 and Source 3)
• Loss of life would be too much (Source 3)

Reasons for rejecting the other option:
A huge majority of people in NATO countries (69%) believe that NATO cannot afford any more missions. (Source 2) This is supported by information from Source 3 which shows that the Libyan conflict cost the UK and USA alone, $21.5 billion without using ground troops.
(3 marks – evaluative terminology, detailed evidence from Sources 2 and 3)

NATIONAL 5 MODERN STUDIES 2015

Section 1

Part A: Democracy in Scotland

1. *Candidates can be credited in a number of ways **up to a maximum of 4 marks**.*

   Possible approaches to answering the question:

   Councils provide services such as education.
   [1 mark – accurate but undeveloped point]

   Councils provide services such as education. They provide education from 3 – 18 in schools.
   [2 marks – accurate with development]

   Dundee City is one of Scotland's 32 local councils. Education is a key service. Nurseries, primary and secondary schools are all funded by the Council. They employ the teachers and people such as janitors to provide the service.
   [3 marks – accurate point with development and detailed exemplification]

   Credit reference to aspects of the following:

   Some pupils may refer to the types of services and should be credited for this.

   Mandatory services – such as schooling for 5–16 year olds, social work services.

   Discretionary services – swimming pools, mobile libraries.

   Permissive powers such as economic development, recreation services; and,

   Regulatory powers – Local Authorities provide regulatory services such as trading standards and environmental health and issue licences for taxis and public houses.

   Councils deliver a wide range of valuable services to their local area. The main services they provide, in addition to their regulatory and licensing functions, are:
   • Education
   • Social Work
   • Roads and transport
   • Economic Development
   • Housing and the Built Environment
   • The Environment
   • Libraries
   • Waste management
   • Arts, Culture and Sport

   Councils also work with external agencies such as the police and fire service to provide community safety.

   Any other valid point that meets the criteria described in the general marking instructions for this kind of question (see column to left).

2. *Candidates can be credited in a number of ways **up to a maximum of 6 marks**.*

   Possible approaches to answering the question:

   People may choose to use the media to influence people.
   [1 mark – accurate but undeveloped point]

   People may join a trade union to protect their rights at work eg teachers join the EIS.
   [2 marks – accurate with development]

   People may join a trade union to protect their rights at work eg teachers join the EIS. They might do this because they feel that they are not getting paid enough money and that the union will take action for them eg talking to their employers.
   [3 marks – accurate point with development and exemplification]

   People may choose to join a pressure group such as Greenpeace because they are worried about the environment and they feel they can't make any difference on their own. Joining a pressure group means lots of people campaign together so they have more of an impact eg Greenpeace have 11,000 Scottish members, this gives them strength in numbers and increases their collective influence on the government. This makes them difficult to ignore.
   [4 marks – relevant accurate point with development, analysis and exemplification]

   Credit reference to aspects of the following:

   Pressure Groups
   • Believe strongly about an issue such as human rights, the environment.
   • Collective action more effective than individual.
   • Media pay more attention to organised pressure groups.
   • Pressure groups have experience of campaigning etc.
   • Seen as the best way to influence government in between elections.

   Trade Unions
   • Protect rights at work eg health and safety, pay, holidays, pensions.
   • TU have experience negotiating with management.
   • TU have legal teams you can use.
   • Collective action more effective than individual.

   The Media
   • Use them to get wider attention for an issue you care about eg newspapers are widely read.
   • Legal way to get attention for your cause.
   • Local and national appeal.
   • Use of different media types eg Facebook campaigns.

3. *Candidates can be credited in a number of ways **up to a maximum of 10 marks**.*

   Possible approaches to answering the question:

   For Option 1:

   I would choose Daisy as she has experience as a councillor.
   [1 mark – evidence drawn from Source 1]

   In Source 1 Daisy says that health needs to improve as lives are being cut short. She is right as life expectancy is less in Glenlochy.
   [2 marks – evaluative terminology with limited evidence from Source 1 and Source 2]

   In Source 1 Daisy states that "The lives of people in Glenlochy are being cruelly cut short". She is correct as Source 2 states life expectancy is only 77 years compared to 79 in the rest of Scotland, a significant difference of two years.
   [3 marks – evidence drawn from two Sources with detailed use of evidence and evaluative terminology]

   Reference to aspects of the following will be credited:
   • Local Councillor [Source 1] – constituents want an experienced politician [Source 2].
   • Source 1 – "I will work to ensure that more women are elected" Source 2 – 54% agree.
   • 54% think the Scottish parliament needs more female MSPs [Source 2] and Daisy as a female would be a good choice [Source 1].

- Source 1 – number of women working locally – Source 3 – only 34% in Glenlochy but 45% in Scotland.
- Source 1 – unemployment a problem – true as 9% unemployed in Glenlochy and 7% in Scotland [Source 3].
- Childcare is a problem [Source 1] – 68% in Source 2 agree.

Against Option 1

Daisy claims a lack of internet access is an obvious barrier however Source 3 shows 3% more households in Glenlochy have access to the internet [2 marks].

Reference to aspects of the following will be credited:
- A lack of internet access [Source 1] – but Source 3 shows 79% have access compared to 76% in Scotland.
- Crime is not a concern [Source 1] but Source 2 shows 530 people attended a local meeting and raised valid concerns.
- Crime is not a concern [Source 1] Source 2 – 65% disagree with her.
- Daisy says health needs to improve but there are fewer long-term illnesses in Glenlochy, 3% less than the UK [Source 3].
- Community council say a legal background is necessary [Source 2] but Daisy doesn't have this [Source 1].

For Option 2:

I would choose Tom because he has experience as a lawyer and Source 2 says our new MSPs should have a legal background.

[2 marks – evidence drawn from Sources 1 and 2]

Tom says that employment is a key issue which has to be improved [Source1]. He is right as Source 3 shows that unemployment is higher in Glenlochy.

[2 marks – evidence drawn from Sources 1 and 3]

In Source 1 – Tom says that "Too few people are in full-time work. He is right as Glenlochy's full-time employment rate is 6% lower than the rest of Scotland according to Source 3. This is clearly a problem, especially as according to Source 2 there is only one major employer in the local area and it recently made 100 people redundant.

[3 marks – evidence drawn from 3 Sources with detailed use of evidence and evaluative terminology]

Reference to aspects of the following will be credited:
- Source 1 – Tom is a lawyer and Source 2 – local people worried about crime would like an MSP with a legal background.
- Source 1 – too few people are in full-time work and Source 3 shows only 42% working compared to 48%.
- Source 1 – many relying on benefits and Source 3 shows 1.7% more claimants in Glenlochy compared to Scotland as whole.
- Source 1 – crime is a major concern and Source 2 shows 530 people attended a meeting to voice concerns.
- Source 1 – crime is a major concern and Source 2 shows 65% of people agree it's a problem.

Against Option 2

Tom claims that a lack of childcare isn't a problem in Glenlochy but 68% of local people think it is a major problem [2 marks].

Reference to aspects of the following will be credited:
- "The majority of local people agree with me that elderly people are well cared for" [Source 1] but Source 2 shows only 35% agree.
- Childcare not a problem [Source 1] – Source 2 68% feel it is.

- Tom says too many are leaving school before S6 [Source 1] – this isn't the case according to Source 3 – 2% more stay to S6 than the Scottish average.
- Many feel Glenlochy needs an experience representative [Source 2] and Tom has no experience as a representative [Source 1].

Part B: Democracy in the United Kingdom

4. *Candidates can be credited in a number of ways **up to a maximum of 4 marks**.*

Possible approaches to answering the question:

They examine government decisions.

[1 mark – accurate but undeveloped point]

The Lords can delay government bills by a year if they disagree.

[2 marks – accurate with development]

The Lords can contribute to government decision making as some of them can hold positions in the Cabinet and attend Cabinet meetings eg Baroness Stowell. Members of the House of Lords have been appointed to other government posts in recent years.

[3 marks – accurate point with development and exemplification]

Credit reference to aspects of the following:
- Provides detailed scrutiny and discussion of legislation due to experience and expertise of members.
- Can amend or reject legislation (limited by Parliament Acts).
- Can introduce bills (not money bills).
- May be able to force government to rethink legislation or policy as opposition in the Lords is often bad publicity for the government.
- Peers can be appointed as government ministers and some do attend full cabinet meetings.

5. *Candidates can be credited in a number of ways **up to a maximum of 6 marks**.*

Possible approaches to answering the question:

People may choose to use the media to influence people.

[1 mark – accurate but undeveloped point]

People may join a trade union to protect their rights at work eg rail workers join the Rail, Maritime and Transport Union (RMT).

[2 marks – accurate with development]

People may join a trade union to protect their rights at work eg rail workers join the Rail, Maritime and Transport Union (RMT). They might do this because they feel that they are not getting paid enough money and that the union will take action for them eg talking to their employers.

[3 marks – accurate point with development and exemplification]

People may choose to join a pressure group such as Greenpeace because they are worried about the environment and they feel they can't make any difference on their own. Joining a pressure group means lots of people campaign together so they have more of an impact eg Greenpeace have 130,000 UK supporters, this gives them strength in numbers and increases their collective influence on the government. This makes them difficult to ignore.

[4 marks – relevant accurate point with development, analysis and exemplification]

Credit reference to aspects of the following:

Pressure Groups
- Believe strongly about an issue such as human rights, the environment.
- Collective action more effective than individual.
- Media pay more attention to organised pressure groups.
- Pressure groups have experience of campaigning etc.
- Seen as the best way to influence government in between elections.

Trades Unions
- Protect rights at work eg health and safety, pay, holidays, pensions.
- TU have experience negotiating with management.
- TU have legal teams you can use.
- Collective action more effective than individual.

The Media
- Use them to get wider attention for an issue you care about eg newspapers are widely read.
- Legal way to get attention for your cause.
- Local and national appeal.
- Use of different media types eg Facebook campaigns.

6. *Candidates can be credited in a number of ways **up to a maximum of 10 marks**.*

Possible approaches to answering the question:

OPTION 1

For Option 1:

I would choose Nora as she has experience as a councillor.
[1 mark – evidence drawn from Source 1]

In Source 1 Nora says that health needs to improve as lives are being cut short. She is right as life expectancy is less in Millwood.
[2 marks – evaluative terminology with limited evidence from Source 1 and Source 2]

In Source 1 Nora states that "The lives of people in Millwood are being cruelly cut short". She is correct as Source 2 states life expectancy is only 77 years compared to 80 in the rest of the UK, a significant difference of three years.
[3 marks – evidence drawn from 2 Sources with detailed use of evidence and evaluative terminology]

Reference to aspects of the following will be credited:
- Local Councillor [Source 1] – constituents want an experienced politician [Source 2].
- Source 1 – more women are elected – Source 2 54% agree.
- Source 1 – number of women working locally – Source 3 only 34% in Millwood but 45% in UK.
- Source 1 – unemployment a problem; true as 9% unemployed in Millwood and 6% in UK [Source 3].
- Childcare is a problem [Source 1] and 68% in Source 2 agree.

Against Option 1

Nora claims a lack of internet access is an obvious barrier however Source 3 shows 2% more households in Millwood have access to the internet [2 marks].

Reference to aspects of the following will be credited:
- Source 1 – a lack of internet access Source 1 – but Source 3 shows 79% have access compared to 77% in UK.
- Source 1 – crime is not a problem but Source 2 shows 530 people attended a local meeting and raised valid concerns.
- Source 1 – crime is not a problem – Source 2 – 61% disagree with Nora.

- Nora says health needs to improve but there are fewer long-term illnesses in Millwood, 3% less than the UK [Source 3].
- Community council say a legal background [Source 2] is necessary but Nora doesn't have this [Source 1].

For Option 2:

I would choose John because he is a lawyer and Source 2 says our new MP should have a legal background.
[2 marks – evidence drawn from Sources 1 and 2]

John says that employment is a key issue which has to be improved (Source1). He is right as Source 3 shows 9% of Millwood are unemployed compared to 6% of UK.
[2 marks – evidence drawn from Sources 1 and 3]

In Source 1 John says that "Too few people are in full-time work. He is right as Millwood's full-time employment rate is 7% lower than the UK's.

This is clearly a problem, especially as according to Source 2 there is only one major employer in the local area and it recently made 100 people redundant.
[3 marks – evidence drawn from 3 Sources with detailed use of evidence and evaluative terminology]

Reference to aspects of the following will be credited:
- Source 1 – John is a lawyer and Source 2 shows local people are worried about crime and would like an MP with a legal background.
- Source 1 – too few people are in full-time work and Source 3 shows only 42% working compared to 49%.
- Source 1 – too many relying on benefits – Source 3 shows 2.3% more claimants in Millwood.
- Source 1 – crime is a major concern and Source 2 shows 530 people attended a meeting to voice concerns.
- Source 1 – crime is a major concern and 61% of people agree it's a problem [Source 2].

Against Option 2

John claims that a lack of childcare isn't a problem in Millwood but 68% of local people think it is a major problem [2 marks].

Reference to aspects of the following will be credited:
- The majority agree elderly are well cared for but Source 2 shows only 35% agree.
- Childcare not a problem – Source 2 68% feel it is.
- John says too many are leaving school before S6 – this isn't the case according to Source 3 – 3% more stay to S6 than the UK average.

Section 2

Part C: Social Inequality

7. *Candidates can be credited in a number of ways **up to a maximum of 4 marks**.*

Possible approaches to answering the question:

The Government has tried to reduce social inequalities by encouraging people to make better lifestyle choices.
[1 mark – accurate but undeveloped point]

The Government has tried to reduce social inequalities in housing by providing Social Housing to those who need it, to make sure everyone has an acceptable standard of housing.
[2 marks – accurate with development]

The Government has tried to reduce social inequalities in education by providing free state education. They also reduce inequalities within education by providing free school meals and clothing vouchers to pupils from lower income backgrounds.

> [3 marks – accurate point with development and exemplification]

Credit reference to aspects of the following:
- **Health:** Passing Laws, providing free health care, issuing public guidelines (smoking/exercise/healthy eating).
- **Education:** Educational Maintenance Allowance (EMA); Student Loans; Scholarships and bursaries.
- **Housing:** Housing benefit.
- **Discrimination:** Equality Act 2010, Equality & Human Rights Commission (EHRC).
- **Welfare Benefits:** the government provides a huge range of benefits for the elderly, families, out of work, disabled etc.

8. *Candidates can be credited in a number of ways **up to a maximum of 8 marks**.*

Possible approaches to answering the question:

Ethnic minorities still face inequality in society because they still face racism in some areas of society.

> [1 mark – accurate but undeveloped point]

Older people still face inequality in society because they face discrimination in the world of work because some employers think they don't have IT skills.

> [2 marks – accurate with development]

Women still face inequality in society because of sexism. Employers, for example, might not want to employ a woman as they think she will need time off to look after her children. This means that women find it more difficult to find suitable work and as a result often work part-time in occupations like cleaning, childcare etc. Many women feel that the glass ceiling still exists which limits opportunities for promotion in their careers.

> [4 marks – accurate point with development, analysis and exemplification]

Credit reference to aspects of the following:
- **Ethnic Minorities:** Prejudice, language barriers, poor educational attainment, higher unemployment rates, specific health issues.
- **Older People:** Ageism; financial preparation for retirement; previous occupation; family support; changes to benefit system, ie bedroom tax and employability.
- **Women:** Sexism; glass ceiling; pay gap; employment in 5C's, childcare availability and costs.
- **Disabled:** Prejudice; over qualification; lack of work experience; family support network; continuing health issues; reliance on benefits.
- **Lone Parents:** Prejudice, family commitments, lack of qualifications, no support network/childcare.
- **Unemployed:** Stigma of long-term unemployment, lack of experience,
- Changes to the benefit system, the recession.

9. *Candidates can be credited in a number of ways **up to a maximum of 8 marks**.*

Possible approaches to answering the question:

The impact of poverty on a child's life

Conclusion – Poverty can have a big impact on a child's health.

> [1 mark – valid conclusion]

Poverty can have a big impact on a child's health. [1 mark – valid conclusion] For example, life expectancy for the poorest children is only 71 years [Source 2].

> [2 marks – conclusion and evidence from one source]

Conclusion – Poverty can have a big impact on many areas of a child's life [1 mark valid conclusion]. Children living in poverty find themselves socially excluded from everyday life [Source 1]. Sixty two per cent of poor families cannot afford a week's holiday compared to only 6% of wealthy families [Source 2].

> [3 marks – conclusion and information from two sources]

Conclusion – Poverty can have a big impact on many areas of a child's health. [1 mark valid conclusion] This is backed up by figures which show life expectancy at birth is 71 years for poor children, compared to 82 years for wealthy children [Source 2]. This is a substantial difference of eleven years.

> [3 marks – conclusion and information from two sources with evaluative terminology]

The Government's progress towards meeting its targets for 2020.

Conclusion – The Government will make little progress in the next few years.

> [1 mark – valid conclusion]

Conclusion – The Government has made little progress toward reducing child poverty in the UK [1 mark valid conclusion]. Source 2 shows us that both relative and absolute poverty will continue to increase.

> [2 marks – conclusion and evidence from one source]

Conclusion – The Government will make little progress toward reducing child poverty in the UK [1 mark valid conclusion]. Currently, a quarter of children live in poverty in the UK [Source 1]. Government made a promise to reduce child poverty to 12% for relative poverty by 2020 [Source 1] but Source 3 shows it will actually be 22%.

> [3 marks – conclusion and information from two sources]

UK Poverty rates compared to other Countries

Conclusion – UK child poverty rates are higher than most other EU countries

> [1 mark valid conclusion]

Conclusion – UK child poverty rates are higher than most other EU countries

> [1 mark valid conclusion]

Currently a quarter of children are living in poverty in the UK [Source 1], this is 4% higher than the EU average of 21% [Source 3].

> [3 marks – conclusion and evidence from two sources]

Conclusion – UK child poverty rates are among the highest in the EU [1 mark valid conclusion]. Only three EU countries have higher rates of child poverty than the UK, these are Romania, Spain and Italy which are all above the UKs rate of 25% [Source 3]. The UK is also above the EU average of 21% [Source 3].

> [3 marks – conclusion and evidence from two sources]

Part D: Crime and the Law

10. *Candidates can be credited in a number of ways **up to a maximum of 4 marks**.*

They can send people to prison.

> [1 mark – accurate but undeveloped point]

They can convict criminals and send them to prison. The Sheriff Court can sentence someone for up to five years.

[2 marks – accurate point with development]

They can convict criminals and send them to prison. The Sheriff Court can sentence someone for up to five years. However, if the Sheriff feels this is an insufficient penalty they can refer the case to the High Court where a life sentence is possible.

[3 marks – accurate point with development and exemplification]

Credit reference to aspects of the following:
- Fines
- Community Service
- Community Payback Orders
- Curfews
- ASBOs
- Electronic Tagging

11. *Candidates can be credited in a number of ways **up to a maximum of 8 marks.***

Possible approaches to answering the question:

Drug addiction can cause crime.

[1 mark – accurate but undeveloped point]

Drug addiction can cause crime as addicts need to pay for their drugs and need to steal to fund their habit.

[2 marks – accurate point with development]

Drug addiction can cause crime as addicts need to pay for their drugs and need to steal to fund their habit. Those with drug use dependency are more likely to be arrested for crimes such as burglary, shoplifting or for robbery and handling stolen goods.

[3 marks – accurate point with development and exemplification]

Credit reference to aspects of the following:
- Poverty/deprivation
- Peer pressure
- Family influence
- Alcohol abuse
- Mental Illness
- Violent media images
- Homelessness
- Poor Educational Attainment
- Social Exclusion
- Greed – White collar crime

12. *Candidates can be credited in a number of ways **up to a maximum of 8 marks.***

The level of public awareness of the law concerning social media

Conclusion – A minority of people know about the law.

[1 mark – valid conclusion]

Conclusion – A minority of people know about the law [1 mark – valid conclusion]. This is supported by Source 1 which shows only 1 in 10 know about the law.

[2 marks – conclusion and evidence from one source]

Conclusion – A minority of people know about the law [1 mark – valid conclusion]. This is supported by Source 1 which shows only 1 in 10 know about the law and by Source 2 which tells us 75% of people, a clear majority didn't know about the consequences of being offensive.

[3 marks – conclusion and information from two sources with evaluative terminology]

- More than half of sixteen to eighteen year olds believed it was illegal for an employer to check social media [Source 1].

Social media and the workplace

Conclusion – Employees now have more. rules to follow about the use of social media.

[1 mark – valid conclusion]

Conclusion – Employees now have more rules to follow about the use of social media. [1 mark – valid conclusion] The Gleninch Council have issued a memo to its employees on the appropriate use of social media during work-time [Source 2].

[2 marks – conclusion and evidence from one source]

Conclusion – A lot of working time is being lost due to the use of social media. [1 mark – valid conclusion] The Gleninch Council have issued a memo to its employees on the appropriate use of social media during work-time [Source 2]. This is obviously a problem judging by the increase in the number of hours lost through social media breaks from half an hour to two hours per day [Source 3].

[3 marks – conclusion and information from two sources]

- Social Media breaks are costing more than smoking breaks [Source 3].
- Social Media breaks have quadrupled since 2010 [Source 2].
- Companies now use Social Media to vet applicants [Source 1].
- The Gleninch Council may sack people for inappropriate use of Social Media [Source 2].

Crime associated with social media

Conclusion – There has been an increase in prosecutions relating to social media.

[1 mark – valid conclusion]

Conclusion – There has been an increase in prosecutions relating to social media [1 mark – valid conclusion]. Source 3 shows a huge increase in successful prosecutions.

[2 marks – conclusion and evidence from one source]

Conclusion – Crime related to social media appears to have increased in recent years [1 mark – valid conclusion]. Source 2 shows an increase in the number of incidents reported to the police from 2347 to 2703. However, police have said that many of these (two thirds) are petty online arguments [Source 1].

[3 marks – conclusion and information from two sources]

- More and more people are being prosecuted for their online activities [Source 1].
- Both the number of complaints to the police and of successful prosecutions have increased [Source 2].

Section 3

Part E: World Powers

13. *Candidates can be credited in a number of ways **up to a maximum of 6 marks.***

Possible approaches to answering the question:

CHINA
Other countries rely on China for trade.

[1 mark – accurate but undeveloped point]

North Korea relies on China for both military aid and for food supplies to feed its population.

[2 marks – accurate point with exemplification]

China now manufactures more goods than any other country in the world eg 70% of the world's toys and 50% of the world's clothes. Consumers in places like the USA and the EU rely on China for cheap goods.

> [3 marks – accurate point with development and exemplification]

RUSSIA

Other countries rely on Russia for gas supply.

> [1 mark – accurate but undeveloped point]

Russia has political influence in the UN. This is because it has a permanent place in the UNSC.

> [2 marks – accurate point with exemplification]

The government of Ukraine wanted to build closer economic ties with Western Europe. The recent unrest in Ukraine was a result of conflict between some of their people, who want to stay close to Russia, and their government. Russia has used its military power to arm some Ukrainians which has encouraged a civil war in the eastern parts of the country.

> [3 marks – accurate point with development and exemplification]

USA

Other countries rely on the USA for military support.

> [1 mark – accurate but undeveloped point]

The US Dollar is like an international currency. Oil is sold in dollars per barrel.

> [2 marks – accurate point with exemplification]

The United States has a 'special relationship' with the United Kingdom, a phrase used to describe the close political and economic relations between both countries. Britain has been the USA's strongest supporter in the War on Terror eg bombing IS in Iraq and Syria.

> [3 marks – accurate point with development and exemplification]

Credit reference to aspects of the following:
- Trade
- Culture
- Defence
- Diplomatic support
- Ideology
- Environment
- Economic migration
- Finance/Banking
- International Organisations

14. *Candidates can be credited in a number of ways* **up to a maximum of 6 marks.**

Possible approaches to answering the question:

CHINA

Some people are poorly represented in government as they are not in the Communist Party.

> [1 mark – accurate point with no development]

Those living and working in rural areas are poorly represented in national government as they are less likely to be members of the Communist Party. The rural Chinese can take part in local committees but these tend to only focus on local issues and not on provincial, national or international issues.

> [3 marks – accurate point with development and exemplification]

Credit reference to the following:
- Income/poverty
- Urban/rural divide

- Gender – national government still dominated by men
- Party membership is limited and has restrictions
- Migrant workers may not be registered and cannot participate
- Those with anti-communist views or those who support democratic reform are not well represented and are often silenced by the authorities
- Pressure group activists are not represented especially if they oppose the Communist system

USA

Black Americans are not well represented as there are few Black role models in government.

> [1 mark – accurate but undeveloped point]

Black Americans are not well represented as they are more likely to be poor. This tends to mean that they are less likely to run for office.

> [2 marks – accurate point with development]

Hispanic Americans are less likely to be represented in government as there is a much lower participation rate among Hispanics. Some have difficulty as English is not their first language so politics and government is difficult for them to understand. This leads to fewer Latinos being elected to high office such as Governor or Senator.

> [3 marks – accurate point with development and exemplification]

Credit reference to the following:
- Low paid unskilled work/white collar jobs. Difference in participation leads to difference in representation.
- Blacks and Hispanics experience social and economic inequality as a result of poverty. Apathetic, no role models, other priorities.
- Women remain underrepresented as they either do not run for office or are not chosen by the big two parties, despite the fact that women are more likely to vote in presidential elections.
- Poorly educated are poorly represented and are less likely to vote.
- Some recent immigrants may not have legal status and may lack representation as a result.
- Homeless people may be unlikely to vote and lack representation.

15. *Candidates can be credited in a number of ways* **up to a maximum of 8 marks.**

Possible approaches to answering the question:

Evidence to support the view of Kristen Nunez

In the USA levels of crime have fallen sharply.

> [1 mark – accurate use of Source 1 but minimal development]

In the USA levels of crime have fallen sharply. A study from Harvard University says there is no evidence which proves widespread gun ownership among the general population leads to higher incidents of murder.

> [2 marks – accurate use of information from different parts of Source 1]

In the USA levels of crime have fallen sharply. A study from Harvard University says there is no evidence which proves widespread gun ownership among the general population leads to higher incidents of murder. This is backed by Source 2 which shows that France has comparatively few gun deaths and they allow gun ownership.

> [3 marks – accurate use of information from Sources 1 and 2]

Credit reference to aspects of the following:
- France allows gun ownership but has the second lowest murder rate [Source 3].
- France allows gun ownership but has approximately one third of the violent crime that Russia has [Source 3].
- USA has the highest gun ownership rate but has less than half the murder rate that Russia has [Source 3].

Evidence to oppose the view of Kirsten Nunez

In Source 1 The Brady Campaign to Prevent Gun Violence found that the US firearm homicide rate is 20 times higher than the combined rates of 22 countries with similar levels of wealth.
> [1 mark – accurate use of Source 1 but minimal development]

Kristen is wrong as Japan is clearly the safest country as it has by far the lowest murder rate and it does not allow guns of any kind.
> [2 marks – accurate use of information from two different Sources]

Credit reference to aspects of the following:
- USA allows gun ownership but has the highest rates of robbery [Source 3].
- Brazil allows guns but has the second highest rate of violent crime and the highest murder rate [Source 3]. Also from Source 2 it has the highest gun deaths.

Part F: World Issues

16. *Candidates can be credited in a number of ways **up to a maximum of 6 marks**.*

African people living in poverty often go hungry.
> [1 mark – accurate but undeveloped point]

During a conflict many people have become refugees as their homes have been destroyed by armed forces.
> [2 marks – accurate point with development]

Many children in countries like Botswana have been left orphaned by AIDS. This has denied them an education and resulted in a lifetime of poverty. Their health will also be affected as they will be unable to afford health care.
> [3 marks – accurate point with development and exemplification]

Credit reference to aspects of the following:
- Poverty
- Ill-health
- Crime/violent assault/murder/rape
- Child soldiers/child labour/child abduction
- Loss of family
- Homeless
- Terrorism
- Piracy
- Nuclear Weapons
- Refugees
- Loss of liberty/kidnapping
- Loss of property/business/job

No marks should be awarded for the identification of the world issue or problem.

17. *Candidates can be credited in a number of ways **up to a maximum of 8 marks**.*

Possible approaches to answering the question:

The conflict in Ukraine has not been solved by the EU as Russia is providing arms to the rebels.
> [1 mark – accurate but undeveloped point]

The UN has tried to stop the recent Israel/Palestine conflict by arranging peace talks. It failed as Israel was determined to stop rockets being fired at its territory and ignored the invitation to the peace talks.
> [2 marks – accurate point with development]

Piracy is a big problem off the coast of Somalia. The NATO naval task force has been successful as it has around 25 warships which patrol the area and protect shipping. NATO ships have reduced the problem but the area involved is so large and the Somali's are so poor it is probably impossible to stop it totally.
> [4 marks – accurate point with development, exemplification and analysis]

Credit reference to aspects of the following
- Libya – success as NATO military power was too much for Libya.
- Libya – failure as tribal/religious rivalries making progress difficult.
- Syria – failure of the UN to agree collective action – Russian veto.
- Syria – the UN have been successful in feeding refugees as they are in neighbouring countries which have offered assistance and are easier to reach.
- Terrorism – success as vast resources committed by NATO.
- Terrorism – failure – religious/ethnic/political feelings are too strong and cannot be easily controlled. Extremists are willing to give their own lives, which is difficult to combat.
- Child Soldiers – War Child has been successful in the Democratic Republic of Congo in that they have accommodated, rehabilitated and reintegrated children who have been displaced from their homes due to conflict.
- Child Soldiers – failure – much of the DR Congo is still desperately poor and still in conflict.

No marks should be awarded for the identification of the world issue or conflict.

18. *Candidates can be credited in a number of ways **up to a maximum of 8 marks**.*

Possible approaches to answering the question:

Evidence to support the view of Ted King

Two aid workers were shot dead in Afghanistan.
> [1 mark – accurate source of Source 1 but minimal development]

Afghanistan is a drug producer and it is more dangerous because two aid workers were shot dead in Afghanistan while the murder rate in the USA (a drug using country) has halved.
> [2 marks – accurate use of information from different parts of Source 1]

Afghanistan is a drug producer and it is more dangerous because two aid workers were shot dead. Afghanistan also has the second highest number of violent kidnappings. This figure is three times higher than for the highest drug using country, the USA.
> [3 marks – accurate use of information from Sources 1 and 3 with evaluative comment]

Credit reference to aspects of the following:
- Colombia has "no-go" areas (Source 1).
- Colombia has highest murder rate (Source 3).
- Colombia has highest kidnapping rate (Source 3).
- All three producers have very high kidnappings (Source 3).

- El Salvador (user) has reduced its murder rate by 80% (Source 1).
- USA (user) murder rate has fallen (Source 1).

Evidence to oppose the view of Ted King

The USA is more dangerous as it has the most drug related crime at 104 per 100,000. This is nearly double the highest drug producing country, Colombia.

[2 marks – accurate use of Source 2 with evaluative comment]

Ted is wrong as the USA is more dangerous. One gang member admitted killing forty people and it has far more serious assaults at 874.

[2 marks – accurate use of information from two different Sources]

Ted is clearly wrong as the USA (not a drug producer) is more dangerous. One gang member admitted killing forty people and it has far more serious assaults than any of the drug producers at 874. The highest figure in the drug producing countries is 100 in Peru which is only around a ninth of the USA figure.

[3 marks – accurate use of information from two sources with evaluative comment]

Credit reference to aspects of the following:
- President says Afghanistan is safer (Source 1).
- Lowest total crime rates are in Colombia and Peru (Source 2).
- USA has highest total crime rate (Source 2).
- USA has most drug crime (Source 2).
- Afghanistan has the lowest murder rate (Source 3).
- USA has the most serious assaults (Source 3).

NATIONAL 5 MODERN STUDIES 2016

Part A: Democracy in Scotland

1. *Candidates can be credited in a number of ways **up to a maximum of 4 marks**.*

   Possible approaches to answering the question:

   Political parties can campaign during a Scottish Parliament election by canvassing. [1 mark]

   Political parties can campaign during a Scottish Parliament election by canvassing. Canvassing gives parties the opportunity to go door to door to speak with the public in an attempt to increase voter awareness of the party.

   [2 marks – developed point]

   Political parties can campaign during a Scottish Parliament election by canvassing. Canvassing gives parties the opportunity to go door to door to speak with the public in an attempt to increase voter awareness of the party. This may secure more votes for the party as the canvassers will outline and explain the party policies to be implemented once elected.

   [3 marks – developed point with detail and analysis]

   Credit reference to aspects of the following:
   - Use of the media – newspapers, PEBs, TV debates, Social media
   - Leafleting
   - Posters
   - Holding a public meeting/rally
   - Publishing a manifesto
   - Use of celebrities to gain media attention and support from voters

2. *Candidates can be credited in a number of ways **up to a maximum of 8 marks**.*

   Possible approaches to answering the question:

   The Additional Member System is a more proportional system. [1 mark]

   The Additional Member System is a more proportional system because the percentage of votes relates to the percentage of seats won by a party.

   [2 marks – developed point]

   The Additional Member System is a broadly proportional system because the percentage of votes relates to the percentage of seats won by a party for example, in the 2011 election the Conservatives won about 12% of the vote and 12% of the seats.

   [3 marks – developed point with exemplification]

   The Additional Member System is a broadly proportional system because the percentage of votes relates to the percentage of seats won by a party for example, in the 2011 election the Conservatives won about 12% of the vote and 12% of the seats. This often leads to coalition governments which mean parties work together providing better representation for voters.

   [4 marks – developed point with exemplification and analysis]

   Credit reference to aspects of the following:
   - Retains elements of FPTP so some direct representation – voters in every constituency know who to contact
   - Greater choice – each voter can contact a number of MSPs due to the regional list element

- Greater choice – two votes at the ballot box
- Smaller parties can be successful, eg Greens in Scottish Parliament

3. *Candidates can be credited in a number of ways **up to a maximum of 8 marks.***

Possible approaches to answering the question:

Support
Some parties, such as the SNP, have experienced huge increases in their membership. After the referendum, SNP membership rose from 26,000 to over 100,000 (S1 & S3).
[2 marks – developed point]

Young people are taking part in politics in new ways such as petitioning, boycotts, demonstrations and online activity such as blogging and internet campaigning (S1). 64% of under18s used social media for information on the referendum (S3). Source 2 also shows 36% of young people have signed a petition, the highest of all age groups (S2).
[3 marks – developed point]

Credit reference to aspects of the following:
- People were very engaged in the Independence Referendum eg East Dunbartonshire 91% (S3)
- 65% of Scots say they have had "lots of conversations with family and friends" about the referendum, compared with 29% who have not (S3)
- Scottish turnout in elections to Westminster was 70% in 2015 and has always been over 50% (S2)
- Participation in the Independence Referendum was high, Glasgow had the lowest turnout at 75% which is a large majority of the population (S3)

Oppose
Younger voters have significantly lower turnout rates at elections than the middle-aged and elderly and since 2001 no General Election has seen more than 50% of young people turn out to vote (S1).
[1 mark – basic point]

Ross Monroe is wrong because in the last three General Elections (2005, 2010, 2015) between 30% and 41% of the Scottish electorate didn't bother to vote (S1) and recent election figures in source 2 show that turnout for European elections is especially low, about a third, and turnout for Scottish elections is below 60% (S2).
[3 marks – developed point with evaluative comment]

Credit reference to aspects of the following:
- Membership of the three traditional Westminster parties (Conservative, Labour and Liberal Democrat) has fallen (S1)
- Participation varies by region: in the Independence Referendum Glasgow had the lowest turnout at 75%. The highest was East Dunbartonshire at 91% (S3)
- Very few people contact their MP, contacted radio, TV or newspapers or went on a protest or demonstration (S2)

Part B: Democracy in the United Kingdom

4. *Candidates can be credited in a number of ways **up to a maximum of 4 marks.***

Possible approaches to answering the question:

Political parties can campaign during a General Election by canvassing.
[1 mark]

Political parties can campaign during a General election by canvassing. Canvassing gives parties the opportunity to go door to door to speak with the public in an attempt to increase voter awareness of the party.
[2 marks – developed point]

Political parties can campaign during a General Election by canvassing. Canvassing gives parties the opportunity to go door to door to speak with the public in an attempt to increase voter awareness of the party. This may secure more votes for the party as the canvassers will outline and explain the party policies to be implemented once elected.
[3 marks – developed point with detail and analysis]

Credit reference to aspects of the following:
- Use of the media – newspapers, PEBs, TV debates, Social media
- Leafleting
- Posters
- Holding a public meeting/rally
- Publishing a manifesto
- Use of celebrities to gain media attention and support from voters

5. *Candidates can be credited in a number of ways **up to a maximum of 8 marks.***

Possible approaches to answering the question:

One disadvantage of FPTP is that small parties are underrepresented.
[1 mark]

One disadvantage of FPTP is that small parties are underrepresented because the percentage of seats which a party wins in Parliament does not represent the percentage of votes they win in the election.
[2 marks – developed point]

One disadvantage of FPTP is that small parties are underrepresented because the percentage of seats which a party wins in Parliament does not represent the percentage of votes they win in the election. In the 2015 General Election, UKIP got 12.6% of the votes (almost four million votes) and 1 seat.
[3 marks – developed point with exemplification]

One disadvantage of FPTP is that small parties are underrepresented because the percentage of seats which a party wins in Parliament does not represent the percentage of votes they win in the election. In the 2015 General Election, UKIP got 12.6% of the votes (almost four million votes) and 1 seat. This is unfair and is a reason why some people believe that FPTP is undemocratic and as a result, do not vote.
[4 marks – developed point with exemplification and analysis]

Credit reference to aspects of the following:
- If party support is spread out and not concentrated in a constituency, parties will find it very difficult to get any MPs elected
- Tactical voting is possible
- There are no prizes for second place
- In safe seats parties have a great power to choose the MP
- Many won't vote for smaller parties in a safe seat
- Strong government isn't always good government
- Political parties often target marginal seats and can be seen to ignore constituencies with safe seats

6. *Candidates can be credited in a number of ways **up to a maximum of 8 marks.***

Possible approaches to answering the question:

Evidence to support (not selective) Morag's view that the House of Lords does need reform include:

Source 2 highlights that the % of House of Lords under 60 has decreased from 22% to 16%.
[1 mark – accurate use of Source 2 but minimal development]

Source 2 highlights that the % of House of Lords under 60 has decreased from 22% to 16% yet almost ¾ of the population (77%) are under 60, highlighting underrepresentation of under 60s.

[2 marks – accurate use of Source 2 with analysis]

Source 2 highlights that the % of House of Lords under 60 has decreased from 22% to 16% yet almost ¾ of the population (77%) are under 60, highlighting underrepresentation of under 60s. This is backed up by Source 3 that shows that 2 peers are under the age of 40 but more than ten times that number are over the age of 90.

[3 marks – accurate information from two sources with analysis]

Credit reference to aspects of the following:
- None of the 790 members are directly elected (S1)
- Women, ethnic minorities and disabled are underrepresented (S2)
- The number of privately educated Lords is 50% which is disproportionate to the UK population of 7% (S2)
- Lord Tyler states that House of Lords was "London's best day centre for the elderly" with members able to claim up to £300 per day in expenses for just "turning up and shuffling off"

Evidence to oppose (selective) Morag's view that the House of Lords does not need reform include:

Source 1 highlights that many Lords bring great experience and expertise to Parliament.

[1 mark – accurate use of Source 1 but minimal development]

Source 1 highlights that many Lords bring great experience and expertise to Parliament in the field of medicine, law, business and science and this is supported by Source 3 which states that the House of lords can be useful when opposing bills in the House of Parliament.

[2 marks – accurate use of 2 sources]

Source 1 highlights that many Lords bring great experience and expertise to Parliament in the field of medicine, law, business and science and this is supported by Source 3 which states that the House of lords can be useful when opposing bills in the House of Parliament. Source 3 also highlights that House of Lords can play a valuable role in scrutinising and revising legislation.

[3 marks – well developed point and accurate use of 2 sources]

Credit reference to aspects of the following:
- In 1995 there were 7% women in the Lords, today about 25% are women (S2)
- Lord Speaker is female – Baroness d'Souza (S1)
- Female members increased significantly – 7% to 25% (S2)
- Lack of enthusiasm for change from both houses as well as the British public (S3)
- Disabled members has increased by 9% (S2)
- 1995 over ½ of the members were hereditary peers whereas by 2016 approximately 90% of members are life peers

Part C: Social Inequality

7. *Candidates can be credited in a number of ways up to a maximum of 4 marks.*

Possible approaches to answering the question:
The Government has tried to reduce the inequalities experienced by Women/Ethnic Minorities/Elderly by passing laws.

[1 mark – accurate but undeveloped point]

The Government has tried to reduce the inequalities faced by women by passing the Equality Act which makes it illegal to pay women less if they are doing the same job as men.

[2 marks – accurate point with development]

The Government has tried to reduce the inequalities faced by the disabled by passing laws such as the Equality Act in 2010 which makes it illegal to discriminate against a disabled person in the areas of employment and education. In the area of employment employers cannot treat disabled people differently and must provide disabled employees with special equipment to help then to their job.

[3 marks – accurate, well developed point with exemplification]

Credit reference to aspects of the following:
- Disabled people are also protected by the UN Convention on Disability Rights (The Disabled)
- Office for Disability Issues (The Disabled)
- Inclusive Communication (The Disabled & Ethnic Minorities)
- The Accessible Britain Challenge & Awards
- Sex Discrimination Act (Women)
- The Equalities & Human Rights Commission – investigates complaints
- Race Relations Act (Ethnic Minorities)
- Women on Board Report (Women)
- Equality Advisory & Support Service (EASS)
- Making Sport Inclusive Programme
- Forced Marriage (Civil Protection) Act 2007 – Forced Marriage Protection Order (FMPO)
- Government Campaigns: One Scotland, Show Racism the Red Card, etc.

8. *Candidates can be credited in a number of ways up to a maximum of 6 marks.*

Possible approaches to answering the question:

Some people have a better standard of living because they have a good job.

[1 mark – accurate but undeveloped point]

Some people have a better standard of living because they have a good job that pays well, such as a teacher.

[2 marks – accurate point with exemplification]

Some people have a better standard of living because they have a good job that pays well, such as a teacher. This may be because they have a number of qualifications, such as a degree, having gone to University for several years.

[3 marks – accurate point with development and exemplification]

Some people are economically disadvantaged because of their family structure. Single parents, for example, may find it harder to find a well-paid job. A two parent family are likely to have a much higher income. Even if a lone parent has good qualifications they can only work at certain times as their child care costs are too high. A family with two parents have a better standard of living, as a result this may have a positive impact on the education and health of their children.

[4 marks – relevant, accurate point with development, analysis and exemplification]

Credit reference to aspects of the following:
- Employment
- Skills and experience
- Number of dependent children
- Education/training
- Poor health: unable to work due to illness

- Racial discrimination
- Gender discrimination
- Criminal record makes it difficult to find work
- Access to healthcare
- Housing/environment
- Inheritance

9. *Candidates can be credited in a number of ways **up to a maximum of 10 marks**.*

Possible approaches to answering the question:

Option 1: Introduce a Fizz Tax on sugary drinks

The Government should introduce a Fizz Tax as Ashley Rodgers states that there is wide spread support for a Fizz Tax on sugary drinks. This is supported by the Factfile which states that more than 60 organisations back the proposal, including the Study of Obesity and the British Dental Health Association. This is further supported by Source 1 when it states according to the British Medical Journal, a Fizz Tax, would reduce the number of diabetes cases by 2.4m and see an average adult lose 3.5kg in one year.

[3 marks – detailed evidence linked from Sources 1 and 3]

Credit reference to aspects of the following:
- A 20p Fizz Tax per litre would raise £1 billion a year for the NHS (S1)
- Tax has been used to discourage smoking and the UK now has one of the lowest smoking rates of 23% (S1)
- One study found that a 10% tax on sugary drinks could lead to a 7% consumption rate. 20% tax would decrease consumption by 15% (S1)
- 35% of people said they would drink less sugary drinks if the price increased and 18% said they would stop drinking fizzy drinks (S2)
- A Fizz Tax has worked in Norway, obesity has decreased from 29% to 22% (S2)
- Sugary drinks creating a 'mini health time bomb'(S3)

Reasons for rejecting other option:

I rejected option 2, not to introduce a fizz Tax, because Source 3 shows that the taxing of unhealthy lifestyle choices has clearly worked in the past so we must introduce the tax.

[1 mark awarded for use of one piece of information with no linking. Do not credit if marks have already been awarded for this point]

Option 2: Do not introduce a Fizz Tax on sugary drinks

The Government should not introduce a Fizz Tax on sugary drinks as 61% of soft drinks now contain no added sugar and the industry is looking at other ways of reducing sugar.

[1 mark – evidence drawn from Source 1]

The Government should not introduce a Fizz Tax on sugary drinks as one study has found that the introduction of such a tax would have little impact on the groups with the highest rates of obesity, those in deprived communities and this is supported as studies have found that consumption on sugary drinks would only decrease amongst the middle class: the poor within society would not reduce their consumption.

[2 marks – evidence linked from Sources 1 and 3]

Credit reference to aspects of the following:
- In the last 10 years the sugar content of drinks has fallen by 9%, but obesity rate have increased by 15% (S1)
- In Denmark the Government reversed their Fizz Tax six months later as Danish citizens simply crossed the border to buy cheaper sugary drinks elsewhere. (S1) linked to source 2 showing obesity in Denmark stay the same at 18%.

- Fizz Tax not supported by the public as Public Opinion poll – 51% either disagree or strongly disagree (S2)
- Drinks industry already started to take action (S3)
- Sugary drinks only account for 2% of the total calories of the average UK diet (S3)

Reasons for rejecting the other option:

I rejected the option to introduce the Fizz Tax as Ashley Roger states this is a common strategy used by other countries experiencing an obesity epidemic that has worked however source 2 highlights that before the fizz tax was introduced in the USA obesity rates were 30%, yet they increased to 33% after the fizz tax was introduced, which is evidence that it in fact does not work.

[3 marks – evidence drawn from two sources, with evaluative comment]

Part D: Crime and the Law

10. *Candidates can be credited in a number of ways **up to a maximum of 4 marks**.*

Possible approaches to answering the question:

The Scottish Government has tried to tackle crime by lowering drink-drive limits.

[1 mark – accurate but undeveloped point]

The Scottish Government has tried to tackle crime by making drink-drive limits clearer by reducing the maximum limit, this means that there should be fewer road traffic accidents, deaths and injuries.

[2 marks – accurate point with development]

Government has tried to tackle crime by making drink-drive limits clearer by reducing the maximum limit, this means that there should be fewer road traffic accidents, deaths and injuries. People are less likely now to drink at all if driving given that the legal limit has been lowered from 80mg to 50mg of alcohol in every 100ml of blood.

[3 marks – accurate point with development and exemplification]

Credit reference to aspects of the following:
- Early release from prison
- Operation Blade
- Anti-sectarian legislation
- Neighbourhood watch
- CCTV
- Speed cameras
- Tags/alternatives to prison
- ASBOSs
- Supervision orders/tagging orders
- Community policing

11. *Candidates can be credited in a number of ways **up to a maximum of 6 marks**.*

Possible approaches to answering the question:

Some people are more affected by crime if they are the victim of a crime.

[1 mark – accurate but undeveloped point]

Some people are more affected by crime if they are the victim of a crime.

Victims of assault may be fearful that it could happen and may be afraid to leave their home.

[2 marks – accurate point with development]

Some people are more affected by crime if they are the victim of a crime.

Victims of assault may be fearful that it could happen and may be afraid to leave their home. They may also have alarm systems fitted in their home, at a cost, in order to try and feel more secure.

> [3 marks – accurate point with development and exemplification]

Credit reference to aspects of the following:
- Business – insurance premiums may rise in areas with high crime rate
- Perpetrators – loss of family, job, house etc should be found guilty/given a prison sentence
- Community – closure of businesses, facilities due to crime/vandalism/robbery etc
- Families of perpetrators – targeted by others in the community
- Some people are more vulnerable to crime – ethnic minorities, young people, elderly

12. *Candidates can be credited in a number of ways **up to a maximum of 10 marks.***

Possible approaches to answering the question:

Option 1: Ban Legal Highs

The Government should ban Legal Highs as legal highs have been linked to hospital admissions for things such as poisoning, mental health issues, and in extreme cases death.

> [1 mark – evidence drawn from Source 1]

The Government should ban Legal Highs as legal highs have been linked to hospital admissions for things such as poisoning, mental health issues, and in extreme cases death. This is backed up in Source 2 which shows that there has been an increase in deaths as a result of legal highs.

> [2 marks – evidence linked from Sources 1 and 2]

The Government should ban Legal Highs as legal highs have been linked to hospital admissions for things such as poisoning, mental health issues, and in extreme cases death. This is backed up in Source 2 which shows that there has been an increase in deaths as a result of legal highs. The increase in deaths has gone from just over 40 to almost 120, which is almost triple the number.

> [3 marks – evidence linked from Sources 1 and 2 with evaluative comment]

Credit reference to aspects of the following:
- These drugs are often included in everyday household products and are often labelled not for human consumption (S1)
- Mandeep Khan states that "more of my time as a paramedic is being taken up dealing with the consequences of legal highs. The misuse of these drugs diverts our attention from cases that are much more important

Reasons for rejecting the other option:

I rejected Option 2 as although Source 2 states 66% of young people know that legal highs could result in death Source 1 highlights that the UK has the most severe problem with legal highs in Western Europe, with significant numbers of young people regularly admitting to taking legal highs.

> [2 marks – evidence linked from Sources 1 and 2]

Option 2: Do not ban Legal Highs

The Government should not ban Legal Highs as in a recent survey, the majority (53%) of 16–25 year olds stated that they had never taken legal highs with a further 10% only ever having taken them once (S2). This is supported by Source 1 when it states that despite media attention around half of young people have never experimented with legal highs.

> [2 marks – evidence linked from Sources 1 and 2]

Credit reference to aspects of the following:
- Control and monitoring of Legal Highs is very difficult (S3)
- Often new versions are created and sold just as fast as the government can ban them (S3)
- There has been little or no research into the long term or short term risks of taking Legal Highs (S1)

Reasons for rejecting the other option:

I rejected Option 1 as although Mandeep Khan states that lots of people are unaware of the dangers of legal highs source 2 highlights that 66% of young people know that legal highs result in death.

> [2 marks – evidence linked from Sources 2 and 3]

Part E: World Powers

13. *Candidates can be credited in a number of ways **up to a maximum of 6 marks.***

Possible approaches to answering the question:

US citizens have the right to own a gun.

> [0 marks]

US citizens have the right to own a gun as it states that they have this right in the constitution.

> [1 mark – undeveloped point]

Australian citizens have freedom of speech. This means they are free to criticise government decisions.

> [2 marks – accurate point with development]

People in China have the right to vote in village elections. This allows citizens the opportunity to elect village committees and village leaders as a form of local democracy. The elected representatives are entrusted with managing local affairs.

> [3 marks – accurate, well developed point]

Credit reference to aspects of the following:

Clear reference to specific aspects of political systems of chosen G20 country.
- Standing for election
- Voting in elections at various levels
- Participating in political parties, trade unions, pressure groups
- Free speech
- Freedom of press
- Protection by the law

14. *Candidates can be credited in a number of ways **up to a maximum of 6 marks.***

Possible approaches to answering the question:

The USA has the ability to influence other countries due to the size of its military.

> [1 mark – undeveloped point]

The USA has the ability to influence other countries due to the size of its military. The USA military is often referred to as the 'world policeman' and has been able to influence countries such as Afghanistan and Libya.

> [2 marks – accurate point with development]

Brazil has the ability to influence other countries due to the fact it is a growing economy and is a member of BRICS. Brazil is also the single biggest supplier of agricultural products to the European Union so is a crucial trading partner. Furthermore Brazil has recently been influential in the "South-South" Cooperation, becoming a donor to developing African countries, providing $23 million dollars to Mozambique to help with the development of HIV/AIDs treatments. This cooperation is seen as being more influential than the "tied aid" models of the past.

[4 marks – well explained point, with exemplification and analysis]

Credit reference to aspects of the following:
- Trade
- Defence
- Diplomatic support
- Ideology
- Immigration
- Culture

15. *Candidates can be credited in a number of ways **up to a maximum of 8 marks.***

Possible approaches to answering the question:

The problem of Crime in Japan compared to other countries

Conclusion: Compared to many other countries there are relatively low levels of crime in Japan.

[1 mark – valid conclusion]

Conclusion: Compared to many other countries there are relatively low levels of crime in Japan.

Evidence – It is one of the safest places in the world to live (S3).

[2 marks – valid conclusion with supporting evidence]

Conclusion: Compared to many other countries there are relatively low levels of crime in Japan.

Evidence – Japan had 22 crimes per 1000 people in 2014 (S1), which is only about one quarter of the EU figure of 80 and lower than all the countries mentioned (S2).

[3 marks – valid conclusion with evidence from two sources and synthesis]

The effects of the changing population structure in Japan

Conclusion: As the elderly population increases so do social and economic problems in Japan.

[1 mark – valid conclusion]

Conclusion: As the elderly population increases so do social and economic problems in Japan.

Evidence – Pensions will be very expensive in the future.

[2 marks – valid conclusion with supporting evidence from Source 1]

Conclusion: As the elderly population increases so do social and economic problems in Japan.

Evidence – Pensions will be very expensive in the future. As Source 1 shows the elderly population will almost double in forty years but those paying tax (15–64 years) will fall to just over 50% of the population.

[3 marks – valid conclusion with supporting evidence from Sources 1 and 3]

Also credit reference to:

Housing is getting expensive as a result of the aging population (S3) 61% own their home, lower than the EU, France, Italy and Argentina.

Japan has a high life expectancy (S3) but this will be difficult to maintain as fewer will be paying tax (S3).

A growing elderly population is listed as one of Japan's problems (S1).

The country most like Japan

Conclusion: South Korea is most like Japan.

[1 mark – valid conclusion]

Conclusion: South Korea is most like Japan.

Evidence – In south Korea the poverty rate is 16.5% and Japan is 16% (S1 and 2).

[2 marks – valid conclusion with supporting evidence]

Conclusion: South Korea is most like Japan.

Evidence – In south Korea only 0·5% more people in poverty. This is the closest to Japan at 16% with crime rate in South Korea also being closest to that of Japan – 22 per 1000 in Japan and 32 per 1000 in South Korea.

[3 marks – valid conclusion with supporting evidence from Sources 1 and 2]

Also credit reference to:

Internet users – 865 per 1000 in Japan and South Korea – highest of all the countries mentioned (S1 and 3).

Part F: World Issues

16. *Candidates can be credited in a number of ways **up to a maximum of 6 marks.***

Possible approaches to answering the question:

Issue: Underdevelopment in Africa

Many people in African countries do not have access to appropriate levels of healthcare.

[1 mark – accurate but undeveloped point]

Many people in African countries do not have access to appropriate levels of healthcare and as a result many people die each year from illnesses such as malaria.

[2 marks – accurate point with development]

Some poorer African countries have inadequate health care with too few doctors and nurses. This makes it more difficult to treat preventable illnesses such as diarrhoeal diseases. Each day over 2,000 children die from diarrhoeal diseases around the world more than AIDS, malaria and measles.

[3 marks – accurate point with development and exemplification]

Credit reference to aspects of the following:
- Unsafe water/poor sanitary conditions
- Low life expectancy/high infant mortality rates
- High illiteracy rates/low levels of education (including attendance)
- Gender inequalities
- Refugees
- Piracy
- Deaths from conflict
- Child soldiers
- Destroyed infrastructure
- Human rights abuses
- Effects of terrorism
- Restrictions to civil liberties

17. *Candidates can be credited in a number of ways **up to a maximum of 6 marks.***

Possible approaches to answering the question:

Some international organisations are unsuccessful at tackling international terrorism because they do not get enough help from member countries.

[1 mark – accurate but undeveloped point]

NATOs methods are unsuccessful at tackling international terrorism because, although they are a very powerful military alliance, terrorists are often not easily identifiable. They are not like a country which would be easier for NATO to fight against in the traditional sense. Terrorists don't wear uniforms and don't stick to one country's borders.

[3 marks – accurate developed point with exemplification]

NATO can't support people who have come under threat from their own governments. Since 2011 they have not been able to stop the on-going conflict between the two warring factions in Libya and as a result they have been unable to protect civilians effectively. NATO is not set up to help install new governments and ensure security and stability in places like Libya, it was only effective in the military conflict against Colonel Gaddafi. After this, NATO members did not want the expense of rebuilding the country in the long term.

[4 marks – accurate developed point with exemplification and analysis]

Credit reference to aspects of the following:
• Lack of training of local security services
• Tribal/Civil War in Africa
• Corrupt government
• Sanctions affect some countries more than others
• The extent of poverty
• Financial constraints
• Lack of cooperation
• Inappropriate aid
• Unfair trade
• Fair Trade
• Increased access to anti-retroviral therapy
• Increased enrolment in education
• Success of UN Specialised Agencies
• Success of Sustainable Development Goals

18. *Candidates can be credited in a number of ways* **up to a maximum of 8 marks**.

Possible approaches to answering the question:

The progress in achieving the world government's aid targets

Conclusion: There has been good progress in achieving the world government's financial aid target.

[1 mark – valid conclusion]

Evidence – In 2014 world governments requested almost $1 Billion in financial aid to combat the Ambiona crisis (S1) and by 2017 almost 900 million dollars will have been donated with 950 million dollars pledged (S3).

[3 marks – valid conclusion with supporting evidence from Sources 1 and 3]

The Central American country most affected by the Ambiona outbreak in 2014

Conclusion: Country Y has been most affected by the Ambiona outbreak.

[1 mark – valid conclusion]

Evidence – Source 2 highlights that it has the highest number of cases of Ambiona at 7719 and by far the highest number of deaths – 3177 – more than double that of country X and almost double that of country Z. This is linked to Source 1 which highlights that country Y has the highest proportion which has contracted the virus at 16%.

[3 marks – valid conclusion with supporting evidence from Sources 1 and 3]

The relationship between the standard of living and Ambiona death rates

Conclusion: The higher the standard of living the lower the death rate.

[1 mark – valid conclusion]

Evidence – Source 2 highlights that the country Z has the lowest death rate at 23% with the highest literacy rate at 83% and Source 3 supports this by showing that country Z has the highest average income of $9876 compared to country Y at $5654.

[3 marks – valid conclusion with supporting evidence from Sources 2 and 3]

Acknowledgements

Permission has been sought from all relevant copyright holders and Hodder Gibson is grateful for the use of the following:

Image © Point Fr/Shutterstock.com (2015 page 4);
Image © Goodluz/Shutterstock.com (2015 page 4);
Image © Blend Images/Shutterstock.com (2015 page 8);
Image © Dean Drobot/Shutterstock.com (2015 page 8);
Image © Mahesh Patil/Shutterstock.com (2015 pages 20 & 24).